AF255654

*On the Five Books
of Moses*

On the Five Books
of Moses

AARON STREITER

RESOURCE *Publications* · Eugene, Oregon

ON THE FIVE BOOKS OF MOSES

Copyright © 2023 Aaron Streiter. All rights reserved. Except for brief quotations in critical publications or reviews, no part of this book may be reproduced in any manner without prior written permission from the publisher. Write: Permissions, Wipf and Stock Publishers, 199 W. 8th Ave., Suite 3, Eugene, OR 97401.

Resource Publications
An Imprint of Wipf and Stock Publishers
199 W. 8th Ave., Suite 3
Eugene, OR 97401

www.wipfandstock.com

PAPERBACK ISBN: 978-1-6667-7838-0
HARDCOVER ISBN: 978-1-6667-7839-7
EBOOK ISBN: 978-1-6667-7840-3

VERSION NUMBER 052523

וְדָבַק בְּאִשְׁתּוֹ

The contributions to this study of Richard Klein
is gratefully acknowledged.

The *Five Books of Moses* is a single book of five sections presented in the following order: **Genesis, Exodus, Leviticus, Numbers,** and **Deuteronomy**. Neither in *Genesis* nor in the first part of *Exodus* is a social structure warranted, because in neither setting is such a structure contemplated. By contrast, as a precious gift, for the second part of *Exodus*, and thereafter for all of *Leviticus, Numbers* and *Deuteronomy*, God fashions a social structure intended to promote spiritual elevation in His Chosen Nation, the Israelites; tragically, because the Israelites pervert His efforts to do so as often as they can; as in one hideous moment He perverts it, and abets catastrophe.

Genesis begins with God's creation of the world, and as an astonishing gift to the last of its elements, Adam and Eve, demands in return only that they obey a single command of no apparent difficulty.

> [26] God said, "Let us make man with our image and likeness. Let him dominate the fish of the sea, the birds of the sky, the livestock animals, and all the earth—and every land animal that walks the earth. [27] God [thus] created man with His image. In the image of God, He created him, male and female He created them. [28] God blessed them. God said to them, "Be fertile and become many. Fill the land and conquer it. Dominate the fish of the sea, the birds of the sky, and every beast that walks the land."[1]
> *(1:26-28)*

Tragically, they disobey almost at once, as their progeny will disobey, and will be punished, as their parents are punished. Free to eat, with one exception, of anything in a stunning cornucopia,

---

1. All quoted text is taken from *The Living Torah: A New Translation Based on Traditional Jewish Sources (The Five Books of Moses)*, translated by Aryeh Kaplan, Moznaim Publishing Corp, New York, 1981.

they eat of the exception. "God said, 'Behold, I have given you every seed-bearing plant on the face of the earth, and every tree that has seed-bearing fruit. It shall be to you for food" [1:29]. "But from the Tree of Knowledge of good and evil, do not eat, for on the day you eat from it, you will definitely die" [2:17]. Almost at once they eat from the forbidden tree, and almost at once they are punished.

At the tree, away from Adam, Eve explains to a serpent that

> [2] "we may eat from the trees of the garden. [3] But of the fruit of the tree that is in the middle of the garden, God said, 'Do not eat it, and do not [even] touch it, or else you will die.'"[4] The serpent said to the woman, "You will certainly not die! [5] Really, God knows that on the day you eat from it, your eyes will be opened, and you will be like God, knowing good and evil." [6] The woman saw that the tree was good to eat and desirable to the eyes, and that the tree was attractive as a means to gain intelligence. She took some of the fruit, and ate [it]. She also gave some to her husband, and he ate [it].
> *(3:2-6)*

Almost at once, they are shattered. God appears, and asks Adam rhetorically,

> [11] "Did you eat from the tree which I commanded you not to eat?" [12] The man replied, "The woman you gave to be with me—she gave me what I ate from the tree."
> [13] God said to the woman, "What is this that you have done?" The woman, replied, "The serpent seduced me and I ate it. "
> *(3:11-13)*

Because, as noted, God created Adam and Eve in His own image, it must be supposed that they understood His command, that they were free to obey or to disobey it, and that therefore the dire punishments they suffer—the serpent to crawl on its belly in the dust, Adam to provide sustenance with difficulty, Eve to suffer in pregnancy, both of them to be expelled from Eden, and eventually to die—are warranted.

As only Adam and Eve exist, concern with social behavior is premature; as it will be as regards their progeny to the age of Noah, by which time God has despaired of human beings, and resolved to destroy them.

As God warns Adam and Eve, He warns the first two of their sons, Cain and Abel, of wickedness they must guard against. Unfortunately, only Abel is vigilant.

> [4] Cain brought some of his crops as an offering to God. Abel also offered the firstborn of his flock, from the fattest ones. God paid heed to Abel and his offering, [5] but to Cain and his offering, He paid no heed. Cain became very furious and depressed. [6] God said to Cain, "Why are you furious? Why are you depressed? [7] If you do good, will there not be special privilege? And if you do not do good, sin is crouching at the door. It lusts after you, but you can dominate it."
> *(4:3-7)*

Because Cain chooses disobedience, he murders Abel, and at once incurs the inevitable punishment he at once finds unbearable:

> [13] Cain said, "My sin is too great to bear! [14] Behold, today You have banished me from the face of the earth, and I am to be hidden from Your face. I am to be restless and isolated in the world, and whoever finds me will kill me."
> *(4:13-14)*

To obey, as history unfolds, a single command, as Adam, Eve, and Cain must do—to live in spiritual probity in the mind of God presumed to be universally known, though long yet from being codified—is to obey God.

Tragically, almost always, and almost at once, people choose disobedience, and are therefore justly punished by God.

That people almost always do disobey Him is established by the fact that in the nine generations from the creation of the world to the appearance of Noah only two obedient people are recorded: Enoch, who "walked with God" [5:24], and Abel. What accounts for the fact, and how God resolves to respond to it, He explains:

[5] God saw that man's wickedness was increasing. Every impulse in his innermost thought was only for evil, all day long. [6] God regretted that he had made man on earth, and He was pained to his very core. [7] God said, "I will obliterate humanity that I have created from the face of the earth—man, livestock, land animals, and birds of the sky. I regret that I created them."
(6:5-7)

Because it is inconceivable that God, who creates human beings in His own image, to which no trace of evil may be imputed, so creates them that every impulse in their innermost thought is *"only for evil, all day long,"* (italics added) it must be that in some unexplained manner they permitted the impulse of evil to pollute their souls, so successfully that only wickedness motivates them; and because He concludes they will never contend successfully against the evil impulse; He regrets that He created them, and resolves to obliterate them.

So He does so; all of them except Noah and his family, because only "Noah was a righteous man, faultless in his generation. Noah walked with God" [6:9]. Therefore, God said to Noah, "The end of all flesh is come before Me. The world is filled with [man's] crime. I will destroy them with the earth." [6:13]

And He does so.

Only Noah and his family survive. But almost at once after a flood annihilates everyone else, Noah debases himself; unexpectedly, given his extraordinary introduction.

He cannot be censured for not warning others of the doom that awaits them, because God commands him to save only himself and his immediate family. He builds, populates, and sets forth on an ark precisely as commanded. Therefore "God gave special thought to Noah" [8:1], protecting him through months of near-total annihilation. And, the ark moored, he "sacrificed completely-burnt offerings" [8:29] on an altar he builds to God.

But then, almost at once, the debasement afflicts him (and one of his three sons):

[20] Noah began to be a man of the soil, and he planted a vineyard. [21] He drank some of the wine, making himself drunk, and uncovered himself in his tent. [22] Ham, the father of Canaan, saw his father naked, and told it to his two brothers outside. [23] Shem and Yefeth took a cloak and placed it on both their shoulders. Walking backwards they then covered their father's nakedness. They faced away from him and did not see their father naked.

[24] Noah awoke from his wine-induced sleep and realized what his youngest son had done. He said, "Cursed is Canaan. He shall be a slave's slave to his brothers."

(9: 20-24)

What sin Ham commits in looking at his father's nakedness is not specified. But that it is, in the opinion of Noah that nothing gainsays, a sin so hideous it prompts him to curse his son, cannot be disputed; and neither can Noah's complicity for facilitating the sin by suddenly degenerating into drunkenness.

That observed, God considers briefly the need for constraint when dealing with human beings; an appropriate introduction to three narratives, all profoundly disheartening, that contain most of *Genesis*.

Thinking of the Flood He inflicted upon an entire world, God resolves,

> [21] "never again will I curse the soil because of man, for the inclination of man's heart is evil from his youth. I will never again strike down all life as I have just done. [22] As long as the earth lasts, seedtime and harvest, cold and heat, summer and winter, and day and night, shall never cease [to exist]."
> *(8:21-22)*

The rest of *Genesis* is devoted to narratives featuring Abraham, his son Isaac, and his grandson Jacob, of which only that of Abraham is even sporadically impressive.

It dramatizes his slow movement from a disgracefully immoral husband of insufficient faith in God to spiritual preeminence.

His abuse of his wife, to which he seems indifferent, for which God does not censure him, and to which he resorts whenever he fears his life is endangered appears almost at once; as does a motif—that of deceit—central to the rest of *Genesis* that pollutes almost everyone connected with it. And his three closing involvements, considered as a unit, seem to render his movement incomprehensible, and thus to void it.

In the brief narrative of Isaac, Abraham's abuse of his wife is replicated. And the narrative of Jacob—by far the longest and most intricate of the three—prompts a question about whether God fulfills a promise to Jacob, and dramatizes, almost to the exclusion of other concerns, the power of the motif, that is, with rare exceptions, destructive.

Though the first words that describe Abram (later, Abraham) bespeak perfect obedience to God, the first episode that features him (and that he replicates often) as is revealed late in his narrative, and as Isaac replicates) is despicable. The rest of his narrative traces his movement from immorality to evolving faith in God, to spiritual excellence. But then it reverts, inexplicitly, to profound immorality, and careens to spiritual perfection, thus seeming to render the movement incomprehensible.

That Abram obeys at once God's command to abandon everything he has known in his seventy-five years—that when God orders him to "go away from your land, from your birthplace, and from your father's house to the land that I will show you," [12:1]—establishes beyond question his obedience to God. But his apparent indifference to his abuse of his wife in the first episode that features him bespeaks a frequent resort to the depravity that prompted God to destroy the world.

When he nears Egypt, forced there by famine, because he fears being murdered, Abram proposes to doom his wife to adultery:

> [11] As they approached Egypt he said to his wife Sarai, "I realize that you are a good-looking woman. [12] When the Egyptians see you, they will assume that you are my wife, and kill me, allowing you to live. [13] If you would, say that you are my sister. They will be good to

you for my sake." [14]When Abram came to Egypt, the
Egyptians saw that his wife was very beautiful. [15] Pharaoh's officials saw her and spoke very highly of her. The
woman was taken to Pharaoh's palace. [16] He treated
Abram well because of her, and [Abram] thus acquired
sheep, cattle, donkeys, male and female slaves, she-don-
keys, and camels.
(12:11-16)

God rescues Abram from his depravity, and his wife from
adultery, by literally plaguing Pharaoh. But of the shame Abram
should feel for what he has done he says not a word; that is ex-
pressed by, of all people, Pharaoh, whose fidelity to God's universal
code of decency underscores Abram's apparent indifference to it,
and God's apparent indifference to that indifference:

[17] God struck Pharaoh and his palace with severe
plagues because of Abram's wife Sarai. [18] Pharaoh
summoned Abram and said, "How could you do this to
me? Why didn't you tell me that she was your wife? [19]
Why did you say she was your sister so that I could take
her to myself as a wife? Now here is your wife! Take her
and go!"
(12:17-19)

Though God rescues Abram, He does not reproach him with
even a word of Pharaoh's warranted reproach.

Neither is his behavior in a series of encounters with God
spiritually impressive.

Though God presents him with an unimaginably bountiful
gift, and seems to demand nothing in return, He finds that His encounters are with a self-centered human being of insufficient faith.

He presents the gift at the first of four encounters:

[2]"I will make you into a great nation. I will bless you,
and make you great. You shall become a blessing. [3] I
will bless those who bless you, and he who curses you,
I will curse. All the families of the earth will be blessed
through you."
(12:2-3)

A moment later in narrative time, He reiterates the extent of the bounty:

> God appeared to Abram and said, "I will give this land to your offspring." [Abram] built an altar there to God who had appeared to him."
> *(12:7)*

Not long afterwards, He reiterates it again after Abram separates from Lot:

> [14] After Lot left him, God said to Abram, "Raise your eyes, and, from the place where you are now [standing] look to the north, to the south to the east, and to the west. [15] For all the land that you see, I will give to you and to your offspring forever. [16] I will make your offspring like the face of the earth; if a man will be able to count [all] the grains of dust in the world, then your offspring also will be countable. [17] Rise, walk the land, through its length and breadth, for I will give it [all] to you."
> *(13:14-17)*

That Abram responds to only the third of the statements above by God about the bounty He has prepared for him is odd; and when he does speak, in the fourth encounter, he seems by no means assured that the bounty will accrue to him: that is to say, that God may be depended upon. Because, he reminds God in that encounter, he is childless, and likely, he thinks, to remain so, he asserts, in effect, that God may not be able to bestow His bounty upon Abram's progeny, because Abram will have no progeny; he asserts, that is to say, that his faith in God to produce the progeny is deficient.

Nor, except for an instant, does the fourth encounter strengthen that faith, though it ends with God terrifying him, perhaps because the four encounters do not convince him; that is to say, because the four assurances do not sufficiently strengthen his faith.

The fourth encounter begins with God assigning the bounty yet once more:

After these events, God's word came to Abram in a vision, saying, "Fear not Abram, I am your shield. Your reward is very great"
(15:1)

To that assurance Abram responds with disbelief:

[2] Abram said, "O Lord, God, what will you give me if I remain childless? The heir to my household will be Damascus Eliezer." [3] Abram continued, [15:2-3] "You have given me no children. A member of my household will inherit what is mine."

God assures him yet once more:

[4] Suddenly God's word came to him: "That one will not be your heir! One born from your own body will inherit what is yours." [5] He then took [Abram] outside and said, "Look at the sky and count the stars. See if you can count them." [God] then said to him, "That is how [numerous] your descendants will be."
(15:4-5)

For the first time, Abram is convinced:

Abram believed in God, and He counted it as righteousness.
(15:6)

But his conviction is gone in an instant. That past, he asks yet again for assurance that the bounty will be his: "Lord, God," replied Abram, "How can I really know that it will be mine?"[15:8]

To that question God responds by ordering Abram to assemble an incomprehensible sacrifice that terrifies him into silence, and commands him to believe that his reward will be very great:

[9] [God] said to him, "Bring for Me a prime heifer, a prime goat, a prime ram, a dove and a young pigeon."
[10][Abram] brought all these to Him. He split them in half, and placed one half opposite the other. The birds, however, He did not split. [11] Vultures descended on the carcasses, but Abram drove them away. [12] When

the sun was setting, God, Abram fell into a trance, and
he was stricken by a deep dark dread.
(15:9-12)

By no reasonable definition of *answer* can God's response to
Abram's final question in the encounters above be considered an
answer. To the contrary; its intent is to preclude further discussion
by enveloping Abram in a trance of deep dark dread, and then, in
effect, commanding that he strengthen his faith in God, or endure
the consequences of not doing so.

When God next appears to Abram, and assures him yet again
that his bounty will be very great, his faith does seem strengthened. But he is still not impervious to doubt.

The assurance is identical to the assurances above. But for
the first time, it is conditional: the bounty will accrue, but only as
part of a covenant requiring circumcision for Abram and for his
progeny forever:

> [9] God [then] said to Abram, "As far as you are con-
> cerned, you must keep My covenant—you and your
> offspring throughout their generations. [10] This is My
> covenant between Me, and between you and you your
> offspring that you must keep: You must circumcise every
> male. [11] You shall be circumcised through the flesh
> of your foreskin. This shall be the mark of the covenant
> between Me and you.
> *(17:9-11)*

Why Abraham (by God's decree his new name) commits to
the covenant is not explained. But it bespeaks, in effect explicitly, that his belief in the bounty God has promised him has been
strengthened; that is to say, that his faith has been strengthened;
because he must presume that if he does something for God, God
will do something for him.

But doubts still linger. When God informs him that Sarai will
soon give birth to his son Isaac, he laughs, incredulous:

> [17] God said to Abraham, "Sarai your wife—do not call
> her by the name Sarai, for Sarah is her name. I will bless
> her, and make her bear you a son. I will bless her so she

will be [the mother] of entire nations—kings will be her descendants." Abraham fell on his face and he laughed. He said to himself, [17]"Can a hundred-year-old man have children? Can Sarah, who is ninety, give birth?" [18] To God, Abraham said, "May it be granted that Ishmael live before you."
(17:17-18)

Sarah, as incredulous, is rebuked by an angel with an obviously rhetorical question for laughing when he tells her she will soon be a mother. The question, "Is anything too difficult for God?" [18:13] continues the rebuke of Abraham also, because his faith is not yet perfect.

It is, however, close enough to perfection in the first of his two profoundly impressive achievements—his effort to convince God not to destroy Sodom, and perfect in the second of them—his obedience to God's command that he sacrifice his son Isaac.

It cannot be demonstrated—and therefore it is only plausible speculation—that the gradual strengthening of Abraham's faith in God charted above is the indispensible precondition to the achievements; that is to say, that the spiritual strengthening enables the achievements.

Unfortunately, between the first and second of the achievements, an event intervenes that seems to void Abraham's gradual movement to spiritual maturity, and that therefore seems to render that movement incomprehensible.

When His angels depart for Sodom, and God refers yet again to Abraham's bounty, Abraham's response is, for the first time, appropriate. As God decrees,

> [18] "Abraham is about to become a great and mighty nation, and through him all the nations of the world will be blessed. [19] I have given him special attention so that he will command his children and his household after him, and they will keep God's way, doing charity and justice. God will then bring about everything He promised."
> *(18:18-19)*

For the first time, Abraham does not ask how, if at all, he can be sure God will do as He says; specifically, how, if at all, His bounty will honor him. He asks nothing because his faith is almost perfect.

Therefore he is, for the first time, at ease, and able to focus upon the needs of others; and to do so with compassion. Specifically, he is fit, for the first time, to plead for sinners imperiled by God's wrath.

When the angels depart,

> [22] Abraham was still standing before God. [23] He came forward, and said, "Will You actually wipe out the innocent together with the guilty? [24] Suppose there are fifty innocent people in the city. Would You still destroy it, and not spare the place for the sake of the fifty good people inside it? [25] It would be sacrilege even to ascribe such an act to You—to kill the innocent with the guilty, letting the righteous and the wicked fare alike. It would be sacrilege to ascribe this to You! Shall the whole world's Judge not act justly?"
> *(18:22-25)*

That not even ten innocent men, the number to which God and Abraham barter, can be found in Sodom is not relevant to Abraham's achievement. Neither is the depravity intended to Lot, to his daughters, and to the angels who rescue them, or that God is justified in destroying Sodom relevant. Only that Abraham is no longer focused only on himself is relevant, and that he pities and advocates for others, even with God; trembling, but insistent. Only that Abraham has gradually become a profoundly impressive human being is relevant.

Had the second, and still more impressive—the supremely impressive—of his achievements, his response to God's command that he sacrifice Isaac, followed his plea in behalf of Sodom, or had the episode that follows not existed, Abraham's movement from spiritual excellence to spiritual perfection would not have been impeded. But that is not the case. What does follow it is an iteration of Abraham at his worst. Suddenly, as though nothing of his spiritual movement thus far had occurred, his disgusting indifference to the abuse of his wife, whom he dooms, as earlier, to adultery reappears:

> [1] Abraham migrated from [Sodom] to the land of the Negev, and he settled between Kadesh and Shur. He would often visit Gerar. [2] [There] he announced that Sarah was his sister, and Abimelekh, king of Gerar, sent messengers, and took Sarah.
> *(20:1-2)*

Once again, God warns, but confirms:

> [3] God came to Abimelekh in a dream that night. "You will die because of the woman you took," He said. "She is already married." [4] Abimelekh had not come near her. He said, "O Lord, will you even kill an innocent nation?[5] Didn't [her husband] tell me that she was his sister? She also claimed that he was her brother. If I did something, it was with an innocent heart an clean hands." God said to him in the dream, "I also realize that you have done this with an innocent heart. That is why I prevented you from sinning against Me, not giving you an opportunity to touch her. [7] Now return the man's wife, for he is a prophet. He will pray for you. But if you do not return [her], you can be sure that you will die— you and all that is yours."
> *(20:3-7)*

As usual, Abraham's outraged dupe vilifies him in language that reflects his obedience to the universal code of decency, to which Abraham responds in entirely utilitarian language astonishing in its impropriety:

> [11] Abraham replied, "I realized that the one thing missing here is the fear of God. I could be killed because of my wife. [12] In any case, she really is my sister. She is the daughter of my father, but not the daughter of my mother. She [later] became my wife. [13] When God made me wander from my father's house, I asked her to

do me a favor. *Wherever we came*, she was to say that I
was her brother."
(**20:11-13**, italics added)

That the fear of God is embedded in Gerar at least in Abimelekh is indisputable. Abraham's argument that Sarah is only his
sister is duplicitous. That he has been asking Sarah—as a favor!—
to pretend to be only his sister not only once, but *wherever we came*
to a city in which he feared death, is staggering. And that once
again God directs not a word of deserved censure to Abraham is
difficult to comprehend.

And only after his total spiritual regression is recorded is
his supremely impressive achievement recorded: his spiritually
perfect response to God's command that he sacrifice Isaac. From
that command he must conclude, and accept, that, for whatever
inscrutable reason, God has nullified the bounty; that it will not
be transmitted, as He had promised, through Isaac; that it will not
be transmitted at all; and that Abraham himself must nullify the
transmission, by sacrificing the only son he loves:

> [1] After these events, God tested Abraham. "Abraham!"
> He said. "Yes." [2] "Take your son, the only one you
> love—Isaac—and go away to the Moriah area. Bring him
> as an all-burned offering on one of the mountains that I
> will designate to you."
> (**21:1-2**)

Abraham says nothing, awakens early the next morning,
walks with Isaac for three days, builds an altar, and raises his knife
to slaughter his beloved son, the son through whom God's bounty
was to have been transmitted to his progeny, when suddenly an
angel confirms what the process charted above has established:
that Abraham does, beyond question, at last, fear God:

> [11] God's angel called to him from heaven and said,
> "Abraham! Abraham!" "Yes." [12] "Do not harm the boy.
> Do not do anything to him. For now I know that you fear
> God. You have not withheld your only son from Him."
> (**22:11-12**)

At the outset of his spiritual development charted above, Abraham is apparently indifferent to the abuse of his wife, and insufficient in faith. He elevates himself gradually to spiritual excellence so impressive he can plead selflessly with God on behalf of sinners (and is therefore presumably concerned about his wife's abuse). But suddenly, without warning or explanation, he is again apparently indifferent t o his wife. Then suddenly again, and again without warning or explanation, he is spiritually perfect.

Why the two sudden shifts in him occur is not explained. Perhaps they cannot be explained. But that they seem to void his spiritual ascendance is indisputable.

Because the salient fact of Isaac's nature is his unquestioning obedience, he is dramatized only twice: by reiterating the wickedness he shares with Abraham; and by serving as the tremulous dupe in the only scene to which he is central.

The shared wickedness is his cowardly disregard for the abuse of his wife. Like Abraham, Isaac, afraid that he will be killed, instructs her to assert, while they are living in Gerar, that she is his sister. Abimelekh learns the truth, and excoriates him:

> [9] Abimelekh summoned Isaac. "But she is you wife!" he said. "How could you have said that she is your sister?" "I was afraid that I would die because of her," replied Isaac. [10] "What have you done to us?" demanded Abimelekh. "One of us could easily have slept with your wife! You would have made us commit a terrible crime!"
> *(26:9-10)*

As Abraham did, Isaac says nothing, leaving to Abimelekh the censure of his sin, to which he is apparently indifferent; an indifference that seems to prompt God, as it did in Abraham's narrative, to direct not a word of warranted censure to Isaac.

The scene in which he is duped is extraordinarily odd because it need not have occurred as an instance of deceit, and because what of especial value is contested in it is not clear.

What is not contested is the priceless honor of bearing, at God's appointment, from Him through Abraham, through his son, below, and through a grandson, not yet identified by Him.

The first of the appointments was made above, to Abraham:

[2]"I will make you into a great nation. I will bless you,
and make you great. You shall become a blessing. [3] I
will bless those who bless you, and he who curses you,
I will curse. All the families of the earth will be blessed
through you."
(12:2-3)

The second of the appointments is made, to Isaac, who need,
as usual, do nothing to obtain it but to wait quietly for God to
bestow it:

[2] God appeared to [Isaac] and said, "Do not go down
to Egypt. Remain undisturbed in the land that I shall
designate to you. [3] Remain an immigrant in this land. I
will be with you and bless you, since it will be to you and
your offspring that I will give all these lands. I will thus
keep the oath that I made to your father Abraham. [4] I
will make your descendants as numerous as the stars in
the sky, and grant them all these lands. All the nations
on the earth shall be blessed through your descendants.
[5] All this is because Abraham obeyed My voice and
kept My charge, my commandments, My decrees, and
My laws."
(26:3-5)

The third of the appointments is made to Jacob, to whom
God appears on his way to Charan:

[13] Suddenly he saw God standing over him. [God]
said, "I am God, Lord of Abraham your father, and Lord
of Isaac. I will give to you and your descendants the land
upon which you are lying. [14] Your will be like the dust
of the earth. You shall spread out to the west, to the east,
to the north, and to the south. All the families on earth
will be blessed through you and your descendants. [15]
I am with you. I will protect you wherever you go and
bring you back to this soil. I will not turn aside from you
until I have fully kept this promise to you.
(28:13-16)

All four of the participants in the only scene in the *Five Books* that features Isaac imagine they are competing for the relatively insignificant bounty that accrues to a first-born son. All four of them are mistaken; the bounty is infinite, and is transferred at the command of God through Abraham, Isaac, and Jacob to history.

Two opportunities exist for voiding their mistake, or for at least precluding deceit: Rebecca's encounter with God when pregnant, and Jacob's encounter with a famished Esau. Tragically, both opportunities are disregarded.

The first opportunity is presented to Rebecca. Troubled by her pregnancy, she consults God, who tells her that "Two nations are in your womb. Two governments will separate from inside you. The upper hand will go from one government to the other. The greater [the older] one will serve the younger" [25:23]. As she must know, that will occur, because God says it will—because, whoever is first-born, the superiority of Jacob's bounty to that of Esau is immutable fact.

The second opportunity is presented to Jacob, who *is* the first-born, as he can confirm by reviewing, in the presence of Esau, Rebecca and Isaac, the transaction below, that nothing gainsays.

> [29] Jacob was once simmering a stew, when Esau came home exhausted from the field. [30] Esau said to Jacob, "Give me a swallow of that red stuff! I'm famished!" (He was therefore given the name Edom). [31] "First sell me your birthright, " replied Jacob. [32] "Here I'm about to die!" exclaimed Esau. "What good is a birthright to me?" [33] "Make me an oath right now," said Jacob. He made the oath, and sold his birthright to Jacob. [34] Jacob then gave Esau bread and lentil stew. [Esau] ate it, drank, and got up and left. He thus rejected the birthright.
> **(25:29-34)**

Why both Rebecca and Jacob disregard an opportunity above, by speaking up, to preclude deceit, is not explained.

That the motif of deceit debases Abraham and Isaac as regards their despicable treatment of their wives, and debases Jacob and Rebecca as regards their despicable (and, as the foregone opportunities above attest, unnecessary) treatment as regards Isaac in the scene under discussion, does not doom the rest of *Genesis* to a scourge of deceit. Unfortunately, however, the deceit persists, and becomes a scourge at the latter part of Jacob's long narrative, to the benefit of no one's spiritual reputation.

The scene in which Isaac, almost blind, is duped is especially poisonous because mother and son seem equally indifferent to the immorality of deceiving Isaac by lying to him. Jacob, afraid only that he will be caught lying, hesitates. Rebecca, afraid of nothing, initiates the deceit when Esau goes to prepare the meal Isaac requires as prelude to the blessing he will bestow upon him, by ordering Jacob, disguised as Esau, to set the meal, prepared by Rebecca, before Isaac before Esau can return. And she easily dissipates Jacob's hesitation because it is grounded, not in principle, but in the absurd assurance that if his father discovers his deceit and curses him, she will absorb the curse:

> [8] "Now, my son, listen to me. Heed my instructions carefully. [9] Go to the sheep and take two choice young kids. I will prepare them with a tasty recipe, just the way your father likes them. [10] You must bring them to your father, so that he will eat and bless you before he dies."[11] "But my brother Esau is hairy," replied Jacob. "I am smooth-skinned. [12] Suppose my father touches me. He will realize that I am an imposter! I will gain a curse rather than a blessing!" [13] "Let any curse be on me, my son," said the mother. "But listen to me. Go, bring what I asked."
> *(27:8-13)*

Reassured that, at the worst, he will not remain cursed by his father, Jacob follows scrupulously all of his mother's directions, and confronts his ineptly suspicious father an accomplished liar:

> [18] He came to his father. "Father." "Yes. Who are you, my son?"[19] "It is I, Esau, your first-born," said Jacob. "I have done as you as you asked. Sit up, and eat the game I trapped, so your soul will bless me." [20] "How did you find it so quickly, my son?" asked Isaac. "God your Lord was with me."[21] "Come closer to me," said Isaac to

Jacob. "Let me touch you, my son. Are you really Esau or not?" [22] Jacob came closer to his father Isaac, and [Isaac] touched him. He said, "The voice is Jacob's voice, but the hands are the hands of Esau." [23] He did not realize who it was because there was hair on [Jacob's] arms, just like those of his brother Esau. [Isaac] was about to bless him. [24] "But are you *really* my son Esau?" "I am."
(27:18-24)

And thus, his integrity shattered by deceit, he gains what he could have gained, integrity intact, by speaking honestly to his father.

The immediate consequence of the scene may clarify one matter; but other matters are difficult, perhaps even impossible, to understand. When Isaac, by nature a placid man, realizes that Jacob deceived him, he cries out to Esau, unbearably distraught:

[33] Isaac was seized with a violent fit if trembling. "who…where… is the one who trapped game and served it to me? I ate it all before you came. The blessing will remain his." [34] When Esau heard his father's words, he let out a most loud and bitter scream. "Bless me too, Father," he pleaded. [35] "Your brother came with deceit, and he already took your blessing." [36] "Isn't he truly named Jacob (*Ya'akov*)! He went behind my back (*akav*) twice. First he took my birthright, and now he took my blessing!"
(27:33-36)

That Esau's response to the deceit is homicidal is understandable:

[41] Esau was furious at Jacob because of the blessing that his father had given him. He said to himself, "The days of mourning for my father will be here soon. I will then be able to kill my brother Jacob."
(27:41)

That Isaac is not at least furious that Jacob deceived him is difficult to understand; as is his sudden and inexplicable composure when he appears, immediately after Esau exits, to discuss with

Rebecca Jacob's immediate future; for not only has his "violent fit of trembling" vanished, and not only is he listening, to all appearances his placid self, to her wickedness about his marrying, but he is once again blessing Jacob—and in the language of transmission:

> [1] Isaac summoned Jacob and gave him a blessing and a charge. "Do not marry a Canaanite girl," he said. [2] "Set out and go to Padan Aram, to the house of your maternal grandfather Bethuel. Marry the daughter of your uncle Laban. [3] God Almighty will then bless you, make you fruitful, and increase your numbers. You will become an assembly of nations. [4] He will grant Abraham's blessing to you and your descendants, so that you will take over the land which God gave to Abraham, where you previously lived only as a foreigner."
> *(28:1-4)*

Unless he is preternaturally naïve, it is difficult to understand why Isaac does not implicate Rebecca in the deceit in the scene above; or, if he does implicate her, why husband and wife do not—to use no contentious word—discuss the matter.

The scene done, the narrative that involves Isaac ends, God confers the transmission of His bounty upon Jacob, and three dramatic facts darken increasingly the rest of *Genesis*: the introduction and dramatization of a relation between God and Jacob puzzling because God makes a promise to Jacob that He seems to fulfill sometimes imperfectly, and sometimes even to subvert; a lapse of faith in Jacob; and the deceit, continued, becomes a scourge that ravages almost everyone involved in the long closing section of Jacob's narrative. The transmission of God's bounty through Jacob is rendered to him in a vision in a dream while he is on his way to meet Rachel:

> [13] Suddenly he saw God standing over him. [God] said, "I am God, Lord of Abraham your father, and Lord of Isaac. I will give you and your descendants the land upon which you are lying. [14] Your descendants will be like the dust of the earth. You shall spread to the west, to the east, to the north, and to the south. All the families of the earth will be blessed through your descendants.

> [15] *I am with you. I will protect you wherever you go and*
> *bring you back to this soil. I will not turn aside from you*
> *until I have fully kept this promise to you."*
> **(28:13-15)**

The sentences in italics are almost entirely absent from God's otherwise identical assurance to Abraham, and entirely absent from His otherwise identical assurance to Isaac. He promises to support Abraham; but, not as a quotidian matter, only that his progeny will issue from himself and from Sarah. He promises Isaac no quotidian support. By contrast, as the italicized sentences underscore, He promises to protect Jacob virtually day-by-day; thus never in his lifetime to abandon him.

That protection assured by God, Jacob should feel equipped to confront, with perfect equanimity, any inconvenience, any evil, in any guise.

But that turns out not to be the case; God does not protect him when first he needs Him, and protects him only sporadically, or not at all, at subsequent need.

In their first confrontation, Laban deceives Jacob as cunningly as Jacob deceived his father. Laban runs to him, kisses him, brings him home, delighted, he says, with "my own flesh and blood" [29:13] and, deceit in all likelihood already devised, in fact delighted that Jacob, having fallen at first sight in love with Rachel, the younger of his two daughters, who is "shapely and beautiful", and because he in all likelihood unconcerned that her sister, Leah, exists, contracts, because he [29:17]"had fallen in love with Rachel", to gain her by working for Laban for seven years. Jacob is very naïve. Laban is not at all naïve; and perhaps delights in the deceit he contrives for Jacob's wedding night.

Leah participates in it. And in the morning Jacob, infuriated, finding her and not Rachel beside him, explodes at Laban with "How could you do this to me? Didn't I work with you for Rachel? Why did you cheat me? [29:25] Laban's answer is morally rancid: "In our country it is simply no done!" replied Laban "We never give a younger daughter in marriage before the first-born." [29:36]

At the cost only of disregard of integrity, Laban disposes of two daughters rather than of one, and gains the free labor of a son-in-law for seven years more than his son-in-law intended. And so deceit has served him handsomely.

Participation in it has served Leah very badly. She has gained a husband; but a husband who soon hates her.

> [30] Jacob] thus also married Leah, and he loved Rachel more than Leah. He worked for [Laban] another seven years. [31] God saw that Leah was unloved (*s'nooah*), and He opened her womb. Rachel remained barren.
> *(29:30-31)*

At the out outset, Jacob loves Rachel more that he loves Leah. But *s'nooah* means, not *unloved*, but *hated*; and thus, though he begins his double-marriage loving Rachel more than Leah, he soon hates Leah. And Leah knows it.

God also knows it; but nonetheless seems to do exactly the wrong thing. His commitment to protect Jacob notwithstanding, "He saw that Leah was hated (*s'nooah*), and He opened her womb. Rachel remained barren. But because He attends to Leah's needs, and disregards those of Rachel, He assures that neither woman will be satisfied, and that in consequence not even He protects Jacob adequately.

Leah's hope to regain what love Jacob felt for her at the outset of their marriage by bearing sons for him becomes a dreary process of gradual disillusionment.

> [32] Leah became pregnant and gave birth to a son. She named him Reuben. "God has seen my troubles," she said. "Now my husband will love me." [33] She became pregnant again and had a son. "God has heard (*shama*) that I was unloved (*s'nooah*)," she said, "and He also gave me this son." She named the child Simeon. She became pregnant again and had a son. "Now my husband will become attached (*lavah*) to me," she said, "because I have given him three sons." [Jacob] therefore named the child Levi. [35] She became pregnant again and had a son. She said, "This time let me praise (*odeh*) God," and named

the child Judah (*Yehudah*). She then stopped having children.
(29:32-35)

Rachel fares no better than does her sister; perhaps even worse; her infertility underscored by Leah's fecundity, she is so jealous she and Jacob explode at one another:

> [1] Rachel realized that she was not bearing any children to Jacob. She was jealous of her sister and said to Jacob, "Give me children! If not, let me die!" [2] Jacob became furious with Rachel. "Shall I take God's place?" he said. "It is He who is holding back the fruit of your womb."
> *(30:1-2)*

To compensate for her barrenness, Rachel places Bilhah, her handmaid, at Jacob's disposal, and bears, so-to-speak, two sons through her [30:3-7]. Not to be outdone, Leah places her handmaid, Zilpah, at his disposal, and bears another two sons [30:9-12]. Leah bears yet another two with Jacob, one of them as the result of a discussion with Rachel about mandrakes that underscores the bitterness between the sisters is undiminished.

> [14] Rachel said to Leah, "Please give me some of your son's mandrakes." [15] "Isn't it enough that you have taken away my husband?" retorted Leah. "Now you even want to take my son's mandrakes!"
> *(30:14-15)*

Perhaps because God sees no resolution of Jacob's troubles as a husband consistent with both His commitment to protecting Jacob and diminishing the bitterness between his two wives, He resolves finally to diminish the bitterness. Therefore

> [22] God gave special consideration to Rachel. She became pregnant. He heard her [prayer] and opened her womb. [23] She became pregnant and gave birth to a son. "God has gathered away (*asaph*) my humiliation," she said. [24] She named the child Joseph (*Yoseph*), saying, "May God grant another (*Yoseph*) son to me."
> *(30:22-24)*

God has at last placated Rachel, and has thus diminished Jacob's burden. But why He takes so long to do that is not known. Why, despite his commitment to protect Jacob day by day, He does not spare him some twenty years of turmoil is not known. Why He does not warn him even that suffering attends his wedding night is not known.

In His second effort to protect Jacob God acts quickly and effectively.

Having worked for Laban for twenty years, fourteen for Leah and Rachel, and six for some of his flocks [31:41], and having during that time been swindled of his pay "at least ten times" [31:6], Jacob is commanded by God to return home: "God said to Jacob, 'Go back to your birthplace in the land of your fathers. I will be with you" [31:3].

In part no doubt to upend the deception, he devises, apparently of his own volition, a deceitful stratagem for transferring, with Laban's imprudent consent, to himself a good deal of Laban's wealth. To Laban's question, "What shall I give you?" (30:31), he replies,

> "[31] Do not *give* me anything. Just do this one thing for me. Just do this one thing for me. I will come back and tend your sheep, giving them the best care. [32] I will go through all your flocks [with you] today. Remove every lamb that is spotted or streaked, every sheep that has dark markings. [Also remove] every goat that is streaked or spotted. It is with that kind that I will be paid. [33] In the future, this will be the sign of my honesty. I will let you all that I have taken as my pay. Any goat that is not spotted or streaked, or any sheep without dark markings, that is in my possession can be considered stolen. "
> *(30:31-33)*

That agreed to, once again apparently of his own volition Jacob devises a system of mating that assures all of the stronger animals will become his property. But the deceit, it turns out, is unrelated to Jacob's volition; it is entirely God's work, acting in his second effort to protect Jacob with striking effectiveness and dispatch. As Jacob informs Laban's sons,

> [9] "God thus eroded your father's livestock and gave it to me. [10] During the breeding season, I suddenly had a vision. I saw that the bucks mounting the sheep were ringed, spotted and flecked. [11] An angel called to me in God's name, 'Jacob!—and I replied 'Yes.' [12] He said, 'Raise your eyes, and you will see that the bucks mounting the sheep are ringed, spotted and flecked. Let this be a sign that I have seen all that Laban is doing to you. [13] I am the God of Beth El, where you anointed a pillar and made an oath to me. Now set out and leave this land. Return to the land where you were born."
> *(31:9-13)*

In closing, God reveals that He enriched Jacob. And to assure that his departure will be safely uneventful, God appears to Laban the Aramaeam in a dream and says, "Be very careful not to say anything, good or bad, to Jacob"[31-24].

The contrast between the first two of God's efforts to protect Jacob on a day- to-day basis underscores two related questions: Why He devoted twenty years to the first of them, but almost no time to the second; and why His attention wavered from the first, but was unwaveringly focused on the second. Neither question is addressed.

For the first time, because it is the tool of God, deceit is not condemned. Only once more will it be appropriate, the mode of two impressive human beings. Thus, it retains its insidious reputation.

God does not protect Jacob during his reunion with Esau, because there is no need to do so, for two reasons: given God's promise to protect Jacob, that the reunion could be dangerous bespeaks not a possibility, but insufficiency of faith; and that Esau presents no danger.

That Jacob's faith is insufficient is established by the fact that, though God has assured protection, he is terribly afraid of his impending reunion with Esau.

As noted above, "God said to Jacob, 'Go back to your birthplace in the land of your fathers. *I will be with you*'" [31:3]. As he tells Leah and Rachel, "Your father swindled me and changed his mind about my pay at least ten times, but *God would not let him harm me* "[31:7]. Furthermore, he tells them, God has sent an angel to enrich him as "*a sign that I have seen all that Laban is doing to you. I am the God of Beth-El, where you anointed a pillar and made an oath to Me.* Now set out and leave this land. Return to the land where you were born"

Beyond question, God at the least intends to protect Jacob. That Jacob is nonetheless terrified of his impending meeting with Esau must bespeak either that he doubts that intention—that is to say, that his faith is insufficient; or that the experience of twenty years has taught him that God's intention to protect him wavers.

The terror appears first in the groveling message Jacob sends ahead to Esau, then in his reaction to the report the messengers return with, and in the pitiful prayer he offers to God.

> [4] Jacob sent messengers ahead of him to his brother Esau, to Edom's field, in the Seir area. [5] He instructed them to deliver the following message: "To my lord Esau. Your humble servant Jacob says: I have been staying with Laban, and have delayed my return until now. [6] I have acquired cattle, donkeys, sheep, slaves and slave-girls, and am now sending word to tell my lord, to find favor in your eyes."
> **(32:4-6)**

The messengers return with a report that almost unhinges him:

> [7] The messengers returned to Jacob with the report: "We came to your brother, and he is heading toward you. He has 400 men with him." [8] Jacob was very frightened and distressed. He divided the people accompanying him into two camps, along with the sheep, cattle and camels. [9] He said, "If Esau comes and attacks one camp, at least the other camp will survive."
> **(32:7-9)**

And the prayer is disgraceful:

> [10] Jacob prayed: "O God of my father Abraham and
> God of my father Isaac. You yourself told me, Return to
> the land where you were born, and I will make things
> go well with you. [11] I am unworthy of all the kindness
> and faith that you have shown me. [When I left home] I
> crossed the Jordan with [only] my staff, and now I have
> enough for two camps. [12] Rescue me, I pray, from the
> hand of my brother—from the hand of Esau. I am afraid
> of him, for he can come and kill us all—mothers and
> children alike. [13] You once said, 'I will make things go
> well with you, and make your descendants like the sand
> grains, which re too numerous to count.'"
> *(32:10-13)*

Because Esau is not Jacob's lord, Jacob should not, cringing, twice instruct his messengers to call him that. When they return with the news that Esau is approaching with four hundred men he should not demean himself by cowering in distress. And his prayer should not shame itself by the suspicion almost throughout that, because God has done more for him than he merits, He may permit Esau to kill him, his wives and his progeny. But at that moment, as he thinks, of maximum danger, all of his responses diminish him, because all of them bespeak insufficiency of faith.

But there is, in fact, no danger. Though to the last possible moment before they meet Jacob is struggling to protect his family from Esau, they need no protection, and neither does he:

> [1] Jacob looked up and saw Esau approaching with 400
> men. He divided the children among Leah, Rachel and
> the two handmaids. [2] He placed the handmaids and
> their children in front, Leah and her sons behind them,
> Rachel and Joseph the rear. [3] [Jacob] then seven times
> went ahead of them, and he prostrated himself seven
> times as he approached his brother. [4] Esau ran to meet
> them. He hugged [Jacob], and throwing himself on his
> shoulders, kissed him. They [both] wept.
> *(33:1-4)*

Though Isaac predicts [37:39] that Esau will live by his sword, and though unbearably—and understandably—infuriated by the deceit contrived against him by Jacob, he threatens to murder him, when the opportunity presents itself to do so, he hugs and kisses him, and cries on his shoulder. Thus, no evidence exists that Esau intends to murder anyone. To the contrary; he far exceeds Jacob's hope, that "he will forgive me" [32:21]. He does rashly undervalue his birthright. And for some unspecified reason, his wives become "a source of bitterness" [26:35] to Isaac and Rebecca. Those unspecified shortcomings in Esau notwithstanding, why God prefers to transmit His bounty through Jacob, rather than through him, is not discussed.

The difficulty of understanding why God prefers to transmit His bounty through Jacob's progeny rather than through Esau's is compounded by the juxtaposition of the scene above and the hideous deceit central to the rape of Dina. Esau approaches with the murderous bluster of four hundred men who seem intent on carnage, but who in fact intend no harm. By hideous contrast, for the transgression of one man, Shechem, two of Jacob's sons slaughter every man in a city, and his other sons then plunder the city. The slaughter is arranged through deceit. And Jacob's response to it (altered only many years afterwards) is completely utilitarian.

Because his sons are in the field tending livestock when Dinah is raped, Jacob says nothing until they return home and together listen, apparently with only one reservation: to suggest conciliation by intermarriage. Chamor, Shechem's father, proposes the following:

> [8] "My son Shechem is deeply in love with your daughter," he said. "If you would, let him marry her.
> [9] Intermarry with us. You can give us your daughters, and we will give you ours. [10] You will be able to live with us, and the land will be open before you. Settle down, do business here and [the land] will become your property."
> *(34:8-10)*

The deceit devised, the brothers agree, on condition only that all the males in the city be circumcised. All of them agree, and all are in consequence doomed.

> [25] On the third day, when [the people] were in agony, two of Jacob's sons, Simeon and Levi, Dina's brothers, took up their swords. They came to the city without arousing suspicion and killed every male. [26] They also killed Chamor and his son Shechem by the sword, and took Dinah from Schehem's house. Then they left. [27] Jacob's sons came upon the dead, and plundered the city that had defiled their sister. [28] They took sheep, cattle, donkeys and whatever else was in the city and in the field. [29] They also took the women and all the children as captives. They took everything from the houses, plundering all the [city's] wealth.
> *(34:25-29)*

To this carnage—to the hideous obliteration of an entire city for the transgression of one of its inhabitants—Jacob's response is entirely utilitarian:

> [30] Jacob said to Simeon and Levi, "You have gotten me in trouble, giving me a bad reputation among the Canaanites and Perizites who live in the land. I have only a small number of men. They can band together and attack me, and my family and I will be wiped out."
> *(34:30)*

Because the dramatization of Dinah's rape foreshadows the closing section of Jacob's narrative, a section focused almost entirely on Jacob's family dominated in substance by ugly emotions and vicious, even murderous, interactions, and in motif by insufferable deceit, the tone of His buoyant reassurance that His bounty will be transmitted by Jacob and his progeny seems ill-chosen, and that He does not iterate his promise of decades past always to protect Jacob seems ominous.

> [9] Now that Jacob had returned from Padan Aram, God appeared to him again and blessed him. [10] God said to him, "Your name is Jacob. But your name will not be

> only Jacob: you will also have Israel as a name." [God
> thus] named him Israel. [11] God said to him, "I am
> God Almighty. Be fruitful and increase. A nation and a
> community of nations will come into existence from you.
> Kings will be born from your loins. [12] I will grant you
> the land that I gave to Abraham and Isaac. I will also give
> the land to your descendants who will follow you."
> **(35:9-12)**

God's decree that His bounty be transmitted by Jacob perforce materializes. But it begins a long section that spares the spiritual stature of almost no one, and does not protect Jacob.

The section begins with Jacob's incredibly stupid present, and its inevitable consequence:

> [3] Israel loved Joseph more than any of his other sons,
> since he was the child of his old age. He made [Joseph]
> a long colorful coat. [4] When his brothers realized that
> their father loved him more than all the rest, they began
> to hate him. They could not say a peaceful word to him.
> **(37:3-4)**

It is difficult to imagine a father of even two sons insensitive enough not to consider the obvious consequences of rousing even the suspicion in either of them that he is loved less than the other. That a father of many sons would not only disregard such consequences, but underscore them indelibly by presenting—before his brothers!—a gift to the son loved most, is astonishing; especially brothers who, roused to hatred, participated in the destruction of an entire city; and that he would present it to a son haughty, spoiled, and convinced that, by nature superior not only to his brothers, but also his father, his father's gift, is nothing more than he deserves—in two dreams, which he thoughtfully parses!

Both of them of course intensify his brothers' hatred, and startle and worry the father; as they should, the meaning of both being obviously the same, and, for in the first dream they were, he says "binding sheaves in the field, when my sheaf suddenly stood up erect. Your sheaves formed a circle around my sheaf, and bowed down to it." [37:6-7] "Do you want to be our king?" retorted the brothers? "Do you intend to rule over us?"[37:8] And in the second dream "the sun, the moon, and eleven stars were bowing down to me".[37:9]

Whether or not Joseph's dreams are prophetic and thus emanate from God is not clear. If they are, why God is leading Joseph towards possibly even lethal danger, and towards the profoundly disturbing consequences of His doing so that accrue through the rest of *Genesis* is a perplexing question that is not addressed.

The consequence Joseph's brothers intend for Joseph's insensitivity regarding his dreams is the same as they intend for Jacob's insensitivity regarding the colorful coat. The consequence is the murder of Joseph.

They attempt it promptly.

When they see him approaching from afar, sent by Jacob to visit them, all but Reuben and Judah agree to kill him; though, it turns out, they lack the stomach for fratricide:

> [18] They saw him in the distance, and before he reached them, they were plotting to kill him. [19] "Here comes the dreamer!" they said to one another. [20] "Now we have the chance! Let's kill him and throw him into one of the wells. We can say that a wild beast ate him. Then let's see what will become of his dreams!" [21] Reuben heard these words and tried to rescue [Joseph]. "Let's not kill him!" he said.[22] Reuben tried to reason with his brothers. "Don't commit bloodshed. You can throw him into this well in the desert, and you won't have to lay a hand on him." His plan was to rescue [Joseph] from [his brothers] and bring him back to his father. [23] When Joseph came to his brothers, they stripped him of the long colorful coat that he was wearing. [24] They took him and threw him into the well. The well was empty; there was no water in it.
>
> *(37:18-24)*

Had the brothers other than Reuben and Judah been adamant about fratricide, they would have insisted upon their original plan: that Joseph first be murdered, his corpse then thrown into a well; or, had they been squeamish only about shedding blood,

Reuben seemed to offer the option of Joseph dying in the well, no blood shed.

That neither Judah nor Reuben wants Joseph murdered is certain.

when a caravan passes:

> [25] The [brothers] sat down and ate a meal. When they looked up, they saw an Arab caravan coming from Gilead. The camels were carrying gum, balsam, and resin, transporting them to Egypt. [26] Judah said to his brothers, "What will we gain if we kill our brother and cover his blood? [27] Let's sell him to the Arabs and not harm him with our own hands. After all, he's our brother, our own flesh and blood." His brothers agreed.
> *(37:25-27)*

Why, though infuriated, Judah's brothers agree at once to his plan for ridding themselves of Joseph, is not discussed. Whatever the reasons, to extenuate their behavior in any way is to demean virtue, for two reasons. The first is that Joseph is their brother, their own flesh and blood, and that they want him dead not because he has harmed them in any tangible way, but because their father loves him more he loves them, and stupidly shows it, and because he is insufferably insensitive, and that therefore a murderous storm of jealousy and hatred has been roused in them. The second is that the crucial consequence to themselves and to their father of their behavior is that it occasions the most important instance of deceit in *Genesis*—the deceit that is the longest maintained, that dominates and darkens profoundly the narrative it inhabits, and that devastates twenty-two of the closing years of Jacob's life.

The consequence is dormant only so that it can be condemned by juxtaposition to its spiritual opposite, and then so that the indispensible prelude to its unfolding, the social ascent in Egypt of Joseph, can be dramatized. Thereafter, its dominance is unchallenged. The juxtaposition is that between the hideous deceit fashioned by Joseph's brothers (including Reuben and Judah) and maintained by them for more than two decades—the fiction that a wild animal killed Joseph—and Judah's response to the only instance in *Genesis* of a deceit fashioned by human beings that is morally justified.

The news of Joseph's death, proven to Jacob by the ghoulish display of his blood-drenched colorful coat, devastates him, as beyond question the brothers intend it to do:

> [31] [The brothers] took Joseph's coat. They slaughtered a goat and dipped the coat in the blood. [32] They sent the long colorful coat, and it was brought to their father. "We found this," explained [the brothers when they returned]."Try to identify it. Is it your son's coat or not?" [33] [Jacob immediately] recognized it. "It is my son's coat!" he cried! "A wild beast must have eaten him!" My Joseph has been torn to pieces!" [34] He tore his robes in grief and put on sackcloth. He kept himself in mourning for many days. [35] All his sons and daughters tried to console him, but he refused to be comforted. "I will go down to the grave mourning for my son," he said. He wept for [his son] as only a father could.
> *(37:31-35)*

Even the abject cowardice of having the coat brought to Jacob, rather than bringing it to him themselves, is loathsome; as is the pretense that they are not sure whose coat is before them; as is the canard that they try to console him; as is their vicious delight, virtually undisguised, in compounding his unbearable pain. And through the twenty-two years he mourns, without relieve, all of the brothers maintain their deceit, uttering not a word of hope to their father, not a word even to themselves of stricken conscience, not a word that bespeaks intent ever to abandon their deceit.[2]

By absolute contrast, the deceitful relationship that enmeshes Judah and Tamar elevates both of them spiritually.

Because the first- and second-born of Judah's three sons offend God, He kills them. Afraid that God will kill his youngest son also, Judah deceives Tamar, the widow of his eldest son. She, in

---

2. When Joseph is introduced (37:2) he is 17. When he interprets Pharaoh's dreams (41:1-46) he is 30. Through seven years of plenty (41:47) and the first two years of famine (45:6) he is Pharaoh's vicegerent in Egypt. Then Jacob comes to Egypt. Thus, he and Joseph have been separated for 22 years.

turn, deceives him. But the double deceit uncovered, Judah admits that his resort to deceit was culpable, whereas hers was justified. Thus, for the only time in *Genesis,* deceit fosters virtue in human beings.

> [6] Judah took a wife for Er his first-born, and her name was Tamar. [7] Judah's first-born Er was evil in God's eyes, and God made him die. [8] Judah said to Onan [his second-born], "Marry your brother's wife, and thus fulfill the duty of a brother-in-law to her. You will thus raise children to keep your [brother's] name alive." [9] Onan, however, realized that the children would not carry his name. Therefore, whenever he came to his brother's wife, he let [the seed] go to waste on the ground, so as not to have children in his brother's name. [10] What he did was evil in God's eyes, and He also made him die. [11] Judah said to his daughter-in-law Tamar, "Live as a widow in your father's house until my son Shelah is grown." He was putting her off because he was concerned that [Shelah], too, would die like his brothers. Tamar left and lived in her father's house.
> *(38:6-11)*

At some unspecified point during the "long time" [38:12] that then passes, Tamar must realize that Judah is deceiving her, and is probably intent on "putting her off " forever. Therefore she fashions her own deceit. Aware that Judah has lost his wife,

> [14] She took off her widow's garb, and covered herself with a veil. Thus disguised, she sat at the entrance of Twin Wells (*eynayim*) on the road to Timna. She had seen that Shelah was grown, and she had not been given to him as a wife. [15] Judah saw her, and because she had covered her face, he assumed that she was a prostitute. [16] He turned aside to her on the road, not knowing that she was his own daughter-in-law. "Hello there," he said. "Let me come to you." "What will you give me if you come to me?" [17] "I will send you a kid from the flock." "But you must give me something of security until you send it." [18] "What do you want for security?" "Your seal, your

wrap, and the staff in your hand," she replied. He gave
them to her and came to her, making her pregnant.
[19] She got up and left, taking off her veil and putting
her widow's garb back on.
(38: 14-19)

When Judah discovers soon afterward that, because she cannot be located, he cannot pay the prostitute her wage, he is puzzled.
When he discovers three months after the encounter with her that
his daughter-in-law is pregnant, he is so infuriated that he orders
she be burnt to death in public. But he renounces that injustice because she confronts him with exquisite tact, and because he admits
at once that he, and therefore his resort to deceit, were culpable,
and that she and hers just.

> [24] Some three months passed, and Judah was told,
> "Your daughter-in-law has been behaving loosely. She
> has become pregnant from her looseness." "Take her out
> and have her burned," said Judah. [25] When she was be-
> ing taken out, she sent [the security] to her father-in-law
> with the message, "I am pregnant by the man who is the
> owner of these articles." [When Judah came to her,] she
> said, "If you would, identify [these objects]. Who is the
> owner of this seal, this wrap, and this staff?" [26] Judah
> immediately recognized them. "She is more innocent
> than I am!" he said. She did it because I did not give her
> my son Shelah." He was not intimate with her anymore.
> *(38:24-26)*

She could have exhibited Judah's securities in public and ar-
gued that, as a widow, she had done nothing punishable by death;
indeed, nothing in any way punishable. But in public she says,
and does, nothing. She acts, instead, only as she is being taken
out, presumably to be burned to death, by a message she sends
to Judah only; at grave danger to herself, because he could simply
have refused to associate the message with himself, or simply have
disposed of the seal, the wrap, and the staff. That is to say, he could
have maintained his deceit at the spiritual cost of knowing that he
had murdered his daughter-in-law.

That, instead, he confesses publically to what he did, perhaps understandably because only in the hope of safeguarding the life of the last of his remainin sons, bespeaks Judah's spiritual stature, and the capacity of deceit to elevate spiritually. The behavior of Tamar bespeaks the same stature.

Unfortunately, no other human encounter in *Genesis* bespeaks that. In all other relevant encounters, deceit bespeaks profoundly disheartening spiritual deficiency. And only the encounter between Judah and Tamar rebukes them.

It does so with especial force in the encounter between Joseph and his brothers, because that encounter and the encounter between Judah and Tamar are juxtaposed. The juxtaposition dramatized, and the indispensible prelude to Joseph's treatment of his brothers provided—his years in prison, his interpretation there of the dreams of Pharaoh's steward and baker, his interpretations in consequence of two of Pharaoh's dreams, his elevation in consequence of that to Pharaoh's vicegerent, and his wait through seven years for his brothers to arrive in Egypt—Joseph's elaborate deceit unfolds. Its unmistakable intent—to torture his brothers—perforce succeeds without effort, because he is Pharaoh's vicegerent, and they are strangers from a country struck by famine desperate to buy food. And no evidence exists that he ever considers the obvious fact that torturing them inescapably entails torturing his father, who has never inentionally offended him.

He attacks his brothers at once:

> [8] Joseph recognized his brothers, but they did not recognize him. [9] He remembered what he had dreamed about him. "You are spies!" he said to them. "You have come to see where the land is exposed to attack." [10] "No my lord!" they replied. "We are your servants who have come only to buy food. [11] We are all the sons of the same man. We are honorable men. We would never think of being spies."
> *(42:8-11)*

Their protestations Joseph dismisses as nonsense; and hearing the two brothers are not present, one of them dead, he demands that the other, the youngest of the twelve, be brought to him, as the only proof he will accept that they are not spies. He demands that one of them return home, and return with the youngest brother. Then he imprisons all of them for three days, and revises his demand. One brother will remain imprisoned, a hostage. The others will buy food and return home. But they must, Joseph demands, return to Egypt with their youngest brother. Of his death, some semblance of remorse in Joseph's brothers is recorded. They agree to Joseph's demands,

> [21] but they said to one another, "We deserve to be punished because of what we did to our brother. We saw him suffering when he pleaded with us, but we would not listen. That's why this great misfortune has come upon us now." [22] Reuben interrupted them. "Didn't I tell you not to commit a crime against the boy?" he said. "You wouldn't listen. Now a [divine] accounting is being demanded for his blood! [23] Meanwhile they did not realize that Joseph was listening, since they [had spoken to him] through a translator. [24] Joseph left them and wept. When he returned, he spoke to them sternly again. He had Simeon taken from them and placed in chains before their eyes.
> *(42:21-24)*

Though hardly penitents, the brothers feel at least remorse that God is justified in punishing them; and that is perhaps what softens Joseph to tears; though he cries for only a moment, and then continues torturing them, speaking to them sternly, enchaining Simeon before their eyes, and terrifying them by having the money one of them paid for food purchased placed in his pack; which, discovered, rouses horror in all of them that God is punishing them, presumably for their sins against their brother:[Simeon said] "My money has been returned!" he exclaimed to his brother. "It's in my pack!" Their hearts sank. "What is this that God had done to us?" they asked each other with trembling voices *(42:28)*.

Nothing asserts or implies that it was done by God, not by Joseph; or by Joseph at God's behest. It was done, but by Joseph, not by God; and not by Joseph at God's behest. And If he did it to rouse remorse in his brothers, he succeeded. But, that accomplished, he must, as a spiritual matter, relent, by at least diminishing the torture he is inflicting upon them. But he does not relent. He does not in any way diminish the torture. To the contrary; when they unpack at home they are terrified to discover the payment of each of them that Joseph has had placed in each of their sacks.

That torturing his brothers inescapably entails torturing his father, who has never offended him, is evident in the grief that has for many years been tormenting him, and that explodes when, the payments discovered, his sons insist they dare not return to Egypt without Benjamin:

> [35] They began emptying their sacks, and each one's money was [found to be] in his sack. [The brothers] and their father saw the money-sacks and they were afraid. [36] Their father Jacob said to them, "You're making me lose my children! Joseph is gone! Simeon is gone! And now you want to take Benjamin! Everything is happening to me!" [37] Reuben tried to reason with his father "If I do not bring [Benjamin] back to you, " he said, "you can put my two sons to death. Let him be my responsibility, and I will bring him back to you." [38] "My son will not go with you!" replied Jacob. "His brother is dead, and he is all I have left. Something may happen to him along the way, and you will bring my white head down to the grave in misery!
> *(42:32-38)*

And thus they part, Jacob shielded from complete despair by only a forlorn supplication to God, the brothers to renewed terror. "May God Almighty grant" [Jacob] prays, "that the man have pity on you and let you go along with your other brother and Benjamin. If I must lose my children, then I will lose them" [43:14].

And the brothers, led when they return to Egypt by Joseph's servant to his palace, are at once stupefied by terror, and then by deepening confusion. "When the men [realized that] they were being brought to Joseph's palace, they were terrified. They said, 'We are being brought here because of the money that was put in our sacks the last time. We will be framed and convicted. Our donkeys will be confiscated, and we can even be taken as slaves"[43:18]. To this fear an overseer responds oddly, "Don't be afraid. The God you and your father worship must have placed a hidden gift in your packs"]. When Joseph enters, he greets only Benjamin, and obviously moved, quickly rushed out. "His emotions had been aroused by his brother, and he had to weep" [43:30]. And at a meal Joseph invites his brothers to, they are astonished by the order in which he seats them:

> [33] When [the brothers] were seated before [Joseph], they were placed in order of age, from the oldest to the youngest. The brothers looked at each other with amazement. [34] [Joseph] sent them portions from his table, giving Benjamin five time as much as the rest. They drank with him, and became intoxicated.
> *(43:33-34)*

The intoxication perhaps attends what Joseph perhaps knows precludes much more of the torture he has been inflicting:

> [1] Joseph gave his overseer special instructions. "Fill the men's sacks with as much food as they can carry," he said. "Place each man's money at the top of his pack. [2] And my chalice—the silver chalice—place it on top of the youngest one's pack—along with the money for his food. [The overseer] did exactly as Joseph instructed him.
> *(44:1-2)*

The consequence the next morning to the brothers is catastrophic. Stopped by the overseer as they travel homeward, the charge of grand theft proven against Benjamin when Joseph's chalice is found in his sack, they collapse utterly, as though in mourning:

> [13] [The brothers] tore their clothes in grief. Each one reloaded his donkey, and they returned to the city. [14] When Judah and his brothers came to Joseph's place, he was still there. They threw themselves on the ground before him. [15] Joseph said to them, "What did you think you were doing? Don't you realize that a person like me can determine the truth by divination?"
> *(44:13-15)*

Whether or not he can determine truth in that way is considered below. That he can reveal truth by eschewing deceit is demonstrated by the fact that, after listening to a long supplication by Judah, he reveals a cathartic truth. But why he does that cannot be established. Nor can a number of questions raised by the revealing of that truth be answered.

The supplication interrupted rather than done, Joseph loses control of his emotions:

> [1] Joseph could not hold in his emotions. Since all his attendants were present, he cried out, "Have everyone leave my presence!" Thus, no one else was with him when Joseph revealed himself to his brothers. [2] He began to weep with such loud sobs that the Egyptians could hear it. The news [of these strange happenings] reached Pharaoh's palace. [3] Joseph said to his brothers, "I am Joseph! Is my father still alive!" His brothers were so startled, they could not respond. [4] "Please, come close to me," said Joseph to his brothers. [5] "Now don't worry or feel guilty because you sold me! Look! God has sent me ahead of you to save lives!"
> *(45:1-5)*

But which emotions he cannot hold in is not specified. Perhaps he feels that the beginning of remorse in them noted above has roused God's wrath against them, and that therefore as penitents they deserve pity. Perhaps he simply misses them. Perhaps he is afraid, as Judah is, that his toying with Benjamin will kill his father:

> [30] "And now when I come to your servant our father, the lad will not be with us. His soul is bound up with the lad's soul. [31] When he sees that the lad is not there, he will die! I will have brought your servant our father's white head down to the grave in misery."
> *(44:30-31)*

Perhaps he weeps for love of Benjamin. Perhaps he weeps for the perfidy of his brothers. Perhaps he weeps for the tribulations they caused him. Perhaps he weeps because he vanquished them.

Perhaps he weeps because God has vanquished them. Perhaps he weeps at the prospect of reuniting with his father. Perhaps he weeps for any combination of the reasons above, or for any other reason, or other combination of reasons, as plausible, that could easily be noted.

Among the intriguing questions referred to above is whether or not any relation exists between Joseph and God. That such relations exist between God and Abraham, Abimelekh, Pharoah, Sarah, Isaac, Rebecca, Jacob, Laban and Hagar is indisputable. Only Joseph asserts that God directs him; but does not say He does so by appearing to him, by speaking to him, or by telling him in appropriate detail what to do. God *reveals* Himself to everyone mentioned above except to Joseph, who says only that God directs him, but not through revelation.

He does that four times. There is no need to interpret his own dreams; his brothers and his father understand them at once. He does assert [48:8] that God will interpret through him the dreams of Pharaoh's steward and baker, and later [41:16] the dreams of Pharaoh. And he claims that God directs his journey from the pit his brothers throw him into to his eminence as Pharaoh's vicegerent:

> [5] "Now, don't worry or feel guilty because you sold me. Look! God has sent you ahead of me to save lives! [6] There has been a famine in the area for two years and for another five years there will be no plowing or harvest. [7] God has sent me ahead of you to insure that you survive in the land and to keep you alive through such extraordinary means. [8] Now it is not you who sent me here, but God."
>
> **(45:5-8)**

It may be, the information above notwithstanding, that God directs Joseph's journey. But assuming that necessitates the conclusion that God directs the work of a deceitful torturer. That being the case, Joseph's rhetorical boast that "a person like me can determine the truth by divination" [44:15] may be a welcome resort.

That Jacob never asks any of the questions his reunion with Joseph must have prompted is puzzling; questions that pervade Joseph's speech; for example, why, during his years as vicegerent in Egypt, he did not contact his father. Perhaps he does not want to know the answers. Perhaps, himself a master of deceit, he suspects deceit may predominate in the answers. Perhaps, as though *Genesis* were in his hands, he understands that human beings are profoundly disheartening even to God, who, in a gesture He sometime regrets, created them. Perhaps therefore, as though *Genesis* were in his hands when Pharaoh asks only how old he is, "My journey through life has lasted 130 years," replied Jacob. "The days of my life have been few and hard" [47:9]. Perhaps that is more accurate than his assurance to Joseph that God "has been my Shepherd from as far back as I can remember can remember until this day, [sending] an angel to deliver me from all evil.

*

In ***Exodus***, God voids disobedience in Moses (by harassing him) and in Pharaoh (by killing him and a significant part of Egypt), then almost casually ushers in an era of social structure that lasts, tragically, for almost the rest of the *Five Books*. Though Moses initially refuses to serve as God's facilitator to Pharaoh, he agrees to do so. Though Pharaoh initially refuses to release the Israelites enslaved in Egypt, he does so. Though the Israelites, by contrast, sometimes submit to God, they refuse adamantly to accept, except under duress, a regimen whose essence is spiritual elevation, presented for the first time in the *Five Books* as a compendium of laws, and thereby empower catastrophe.

> [3] Moses said to himself, I must go over there and investigate this wonderful phenomenon. Why doesn't the bush burn? [4] When God saw that [Moses] was going to investigate, He called to him from the middle of the bush. "Moses! Moses!" He said. "Yes," replied Moses. [5] "Do not come any closer," said [God]. "Take your

shoes off your feet. The place upon which you are standing is holy ground."
(3: 3-5)

The intent of the wonderful phenomenon is to appoint Moses
as God's facilitator in dealings with Pharaoh. The moment Moses
realizes that is God's intent, he constructs four arguments that
prove, he says, he should not be appointed, each of which God
negates: that nothing qualifies him to address Pharaoh; that nothing qualifies him to introduce God to the Israelites; that the elders
of Israel, assembled, will refuse to listen to him; and that he suffers
from a disqualifying speech defect.

That the four arguments, which God negates effortlessly,
mask disobedience in Moses rooted in deficient faith is not clear
for some time, because a number of events that occur between
the end of his first encounter with God and the end of his first
encounter with Pharaoh [4:17-5:21] obscure the disobedience.
Then, however, it is evident. The contempt Pharaoh heaps upon
God convinces Moses that neither he nor God can contend against
Pharaoh.

> [22] Moses returned to God and said, O Lord, why do
> you mistreat Your people? Why did you send me? [23]
> As soon as I came to Pharaoh to speak in Your name,
> he made things worse for these people. You have done
> nothing to help Your people.
> *(5:22-23)*

That in all likelihood the four arguments convince Moses
that Pharaoh would defeat him is understandable. That he is afraid
Pharaoh would defeat God also—that, indeed, Pharaoh has de-
feated God—would be incomprehensible if his faith in God were
sufficient; as would be his contention that God is inflicting evil
upon the Israelites, who, not having sinned, deserve no rebuke of
God; or as would be the case if sufficient faith had governed his
response to God's assurance that He will defeat Pharaoh not after
Moses' first confrontation with him, but after God has pummeled
him unendurably.

Because God has decided that Moses, though at the moment is insufficiently faithful, is to serve as His facilitator, He silences him as he presents the fourth of his arguments with a rhetorical question: "Is not Aaron the Levite your brother? " He says. "I know that *he* knows how to speak! He is setting out to meet you, and when he sees you, his heart will be glad" [4:14]. That nothing more than that flash of God's annoyance renders Moses at once obedient argues his fitness to confront wickedness far more substantial than hesitance in facilitating.

Because God has doomed Pharaoh, that he is a free agent in responding to the first five of ten plagues and as God's puppet only during the last five of them is immaterial; though Pharaoh's disobedience is gradually diminished by his appreciation of God's power that culminates in theological deference to Him; though Pharaoh's consciousness gradually expands towards obedience to God. He is moved nonetheless, gradually but inexorably, to demolition, because God insists on demolishing him; because, as He says, His glory will be underscored by the process of demolishing him (and, ironically, confounding Him).

As He assures Moses before Pharaoh appears,

> [19] I know in advance that the Egyptian king will not allow you to leave unless he is forced to do so. [20] I will then display My power and demolish Egypt through all the miraculous deeds that I will perform in their land. Then [Pharaoh] will let you leave.
> *(3:19-20)*

Thus, just before the plagues begin, does God underscore, though obliquely, the indispensable prelude to His social structure.

> [3] I will make Pharaoh obstinate, and will thus have the opportunity to display many miraculous signs and wonders in Egypt. [This why Pharaoh will not pay attention to you. But when I display My power against Egypt, and with great acts of judgment, I will bring forth from Egypt My armies—My people, the Israelites. [5] When I display My power and bring the Israelites out from among them, Egypt will know that I am God.

(7:3-5)

Just before the plagues begin, Pharaoh notes that his magicians turn their staffs into serpents as easily as Moses does his staff, apparently untroubled by the irony that Moses' serpent devours theirs [7:10-12]. Thereafter, however, he becomes progressively more attentive to the disparity between his strength and that of God, and finally to the theological fact that disparity bespeaks.

During the second plague, though Pharaoh conjures frogs as well as Moses does, he realizes that he cannot rid Egypt of them, but that he must enlist Moses to "pray to God" to do so. To reciprocate, Pharaoh proposes, unasked, to honor God by letting "the people leave sacrifice to God" [8:4]. To taunt him, Moses asks at precisely what hour he would have the frogs disappear, so that "you will then know that there is none like God our Lord" [8:6].

Against the third plague, that of gnats, Pharaoh is powerless; his magicians cannot duplicate it, because, as they warn him, it is directed by "the finger of God" [8:15]. When the fourth plague, that of insects, occurs, it will taunt Pharaoh, because, as Moses warns him, God will "miraculously set apart the Goshen area, where My people remain, so that there will not be any harmful creatures there. You will then realize that I am God, right here on earth" [8:18]. When the insects overrun Egypt, as though intent on addressing God directly, Pharaoh tells Moses and Aaron, "Go! [You have My permission to] sacrifice to your god here in [our] land" (8:21). Emboldened, Moses bargains for favorable conditions, and Pharaoh once again implores Moses to entreat in his behalf with God [8:22-24].

Nothing in the fifth plague, that of pestilence, or in the sixth, that of boils, underscores Pharaoh's disobedience, because nothing in either plague underscores that for him, as the plagues discussed above did underscore, and as the four remaining plagues will, the spiritual consequence of the difference between his power and God's.

At the outset of the seventh plague, that of hail, the consequence is finally clear to Pharaoh.

> [24] There was hail, with lightning flashing among the hailstones. It was extremely heavy, unlike anything Egypt had experienced since it became a nation. [25] Throughout all Egypt, the hail killed every man and animal outdoors. The hail destroyed all the outdoor plants, and smashed every tree in the fields. [26] Only in Goshen, where the Israelites lived, there was no hail. [27] Pharaoh sent word and summoned Moses and Aaron.
> *(9:47-27)*

As Pharaoh finally realizes, disobedience is a theological fact: sin; at its worst, against God; and that is the only truth worth knowing; worth stumbling towards, through one instructive plague after another; a truth all too often lost sight of in an instant. As Moses predicts, Pharaoh will soon lose sight of it, because "I realize that you and your subjects still do not fear God" [9:30].

His regression is complete when Moses threatens the eighth plague, that of locusts, an onslaught that to Pharaoh's horrified servants portends the annihilation of Egypt, and to ask, "how long will this [man] continue to be a menace to us? Let the men go and let them serve God their Lord. Don't you yet realize that Egypt is being destroyed"? [10:7]

And this time, Moses and Aaron will not bargain, as they did during the fourth plague, for favorable conditions; all of the Israelites will leave Egypt, and Pharaoh will be left with nothing. That threatened, Pharaoh drives Moses and Aaron away, the locusts strike, and Pharaoh accepts, in theological language, total defeat.

Having dispersed the locusts, God hardens Pharaoh's heart yet again, and the ninth plague, that of darkness, engulfs Egypt.

> [16] Pharaoh hastily summoned Moses and Aaron. "I have committed a crime," he said, "both to God your Lord and to you. [17] Now forgive my offense just this one more time. Pray to God your Lord! Just take this death away from me!"
> *(10:16-17)*

The bargaining that marked the fourth plague apparently forgotten, Pharaoh proposes that all the Israelites, children included, leave Egypt to worship God, but that their cattle remain behind. Moses co unters that all their cattle will go with them. Both men explode. Pharaoh threatens to kill Moses if they meet again. Moses assures him they will not meet again. And the most gruesome of the plagues unfolds, that dooms the first-born male of every Egyptian family and of every herd of cattle.

The process by which God nullifies the expansion of Pharaoh's consciousness He refers to often and consistently by the assertion, "I have made him and his advisers stubborn"[10:1]. As noted above, God inflicts the stubbornness upon Pharaoh to underscore His glory.

When, the last of the plagues having ended, Pharaoh drives the Israelites out of Egypt, God continues taunting him. Three days after the exodus He informs Moses that, for the last time, His usual scenario is in place, and will produce the usual consequence, for the usual reason.

As He predicts,

> [3] "Pharaoh will then say that the Israelites are lost in the area and trapped in the desert. [4] I will harden Pharaoh's heart and he will come after them. I will triumph over Pharaoh and his entire army, and Egypt will know that I am God." [The Israelites] did as [they had been instructed.] [5] Meanwhile, the king of Egypt received the news that the people were escaping. Pharaoh and his officials changed their minds regarding the people, and said, "What have we done? How could we have released Israel from doing our work?"
> *(14:3-5)*

In a dramatic moment, their questions moot, the Israelites appear, impervious, as the Egyptians are not, to mass annihilation by God's promise to their forefathers in *Genesis* a family, by the beginning of *Exodus* a people perhaps adamant by nature, disobedient, stiff-necked, contentious, cowardly, averse to spiritual aspiration. And so, perforce, all the Israelites pass through the Red Sea untouched by water, every Egyptian drowns in it, and, appropriately honored, God, though not surprised, is no doubt gratified to hear the ecstatic song of victory into which Moses and the Israelites, first the men, then the women, burst.

But the victory is tragically marred: more than welcome in the destruction of Egypt, but, tragic, in its replacement almost immediately with God's social structure, intended by Him to elevate the Israelites spiritually, but received by them as an intrusion not infrequently frightening, even terrifying, that they accept almost always only under duress, and almost always plot freedom from; as from a God infinitely powerful, who always knows precisely what He demands, never tolerates disobedience, almost always contending with a people therefore, in His opinion, stubborn and querulous.

To this God the Israelites are introduced even as they sing to the miracle that saves them from certain annihilation; but cunningly, so that they do not know the introduction has occurred:

> [1] "I will sing to God for His great victory, Horse and rider He threw in the sea. [2] My strength and song is God And this is my deliverance; This is my God, I will enshrine Him My father's God, I will exalt Him.[3] God is the Master of war, God is His name.[4] Pharaoh's chariots and army He cast in the sea; crushes the foe. [7] In Your great Majesty His very best officers were drowned in the Red Sea. [5] The depths covered them; they sank to the bottom like a stone. [6] Your right Hand, O God! is awesome in power; Your right Hand crushes the foe. [7] In Your great Majesty You broke Your opponents; You sent forth Your wrath, it devoured them like straw. [8] At the blast of Your Nostrils the waters towered. Flowing waters stood like a wall. The depths congealed in the heart of the sea. [9] The enemy said, "I will give chase; I will overtake, divide the spoils. I will satisfy myself. I will draw my sword; my hand will demolish them." [10] You made Your wind blow; the sea covered them. They sank like lead in the mighty waters. [11] Who is like you among powers, God? Who is like You, majestic in holiness, awesome in praise, doing wonders? [12] You put forth Your right Hand; the earth swallowed them. [13] With love, You led the people You redeemed;

with might You redeemed; with might you [led] them
to Your holy shrine. [14] Nations heard and shuddered;
terror gripped those who dwelt in Philistia. [15] Edom's
chiefs then panicked; Moeb's heroes were seized with
trembling; Canaan's residents melted away. [16] Fear and
dead fell upon them, at the greatness of Your Arm. They
are still as stone, until your people crossed, O God, until
the people You gained crossed over. [17] O bring them
and plant them on the mount you possess. The place
You dwell in is Your accomplishment, God. The shrine
of God Your hands have founded. [18] God will reign
forever and ever."
(*15:1-18*)

That the consequence of so profound and heart-felt a tribute
to God would be permanent, or at least long-lasting, gratitude to
Him seems self-evident. Tragically, however, that is not the consequence. To the contrary; within three days the Israelites are whining to Moses as though God had never split a sea to rescue them
from certain death, and as though they had never sung a heart-felt
tribute to Him for splitting it. And they are complaining about
nothing more than bitterness in their water; as though God could
not, or would not, sweeten water for them; and soon thereafter, the
water sweetened, about starving; as though He could not, or would
not, feed them; though He does.

> [22] Moses led the Israelites away from the Red Sea, and
> they went out into the Shur Desert. They traveled for
> three days in the desert without finding any water. [23]
> Finally, they came to Marah, but they could not drink any
> water there. The water was bitter (*marah*), and that was
> why the place was called Marah. [24] The people com-
> plained to Moses. What shall we drink? They demanded.
> [25] When [Moses] cried out to God, He showed him
> a certain tree. [Moses] threw it into the water, and the
> water became drinkable. It was there that [God] taught
> them survival techniques and methods, and there he
> tested them. [26] *He said, "If you obey God your Lord,*
> *and do what is upright in His eyes, carefully heeding all*
> *His commandments and keeping all of His decrees, then I*

> *will not strike you with any of the sicknesses that I brought
> on Egypt."*
> (**15:22-26,** italics added)

And soon thereafter, in the desert of Sin, they erupt again, an entire nation enraged at being, in its shamefully ungrateful opinion, maliciously starved to death:

> [2] There in the desert, the entire Israelite community began to complain against Moses and Aaron. [3] The Israelites said to them, "If only we had died by God's hand in Egypt! There at least we could sit by pots of meat and eat our fill of bread! But you had to bring us out into this desert, to kill the entire community by starvation!"[4] God said to Moses, "I will make bread rain to you from the sky. The people will go out and gather enough for each day. *I will test them to see whether or not they will keep My law. (italics added)* [5] On Friday, they will have to prepare what they bring home. It will be twice as much as they gather every other day."
> (*16:2-5*)

Because the whining in both places establishes that miracles alone are insufficient to promote in the Israelites enduring, or even short-term, obedience; that for spiritual elevation in them a complement to miracles is required. And God has already provided it: a complement that, one exposure aside, is foreign to them, introduced suddenly, almost stealthily: a compendium of laws comprehensive, intricate, and difficult, that complements miracles, because miracles alone require only passive acceptance as gifts, whereas the complement requires an ongoing interchange with God, who has mandated the laws.

How aware, if at all, the Israelites are of what they are consenting to when they accept, without comment, the complement contained in the italicized material above is not clear, because, as noted above, they were exposed to it only once before, during the night they left Egypt. On that night, the first of what must seem to the Israelites an endless number of—and is in fact several hundreds of—a compendium of—rules and regulations imposed forever:

[1] God said to Moses and Aaron in Egypt, [2]"This month shall be the head month to you. It shall be the first month of the year. [3] Speak to the entire congregation of Israel, saying: On the tenth of this month, every man must take a lamb for each extended family, a lamb for each household. [4] If the household is too small for a lamb, then he and a close neighbor can obtain a [lamb together], as long as it is for specifically designated individuals. Individuals shall be designated a lamb according to how much each one will eat. [5] You must have a flawless young animal, a one-year-old male. You can take it from the sheep or from the goats. [6] Hold it is safekeeping until the fourteenth day of this month. The entire community of Israel shall then slaughter [their sacrifices] in the afternoon. [7] They must take the blood and place it on the two doorposts and on the beam above the door of the houses in which they will eat [the sacrifice]. [8] Eat the [sacrificial] meat during the night roasted over the fire. Eat it with matzah and bitter herbs. [9] Do not eat it raw or cooked in water, but only roasted over fire, including its head, is legs, and its internal organs. [10] Do not leave any of it over until morning. Anything that is left over until morning must be burned in fire. [11] You must eat it with your waist belted, your shoes on your feet, and your staff in your hand, and you must eat in haste. It is the Passover (*Pesach*) offering to God."
(12:1-11)

At Marah, they want water, but almost certainly not a binding contract with God. At Sin they want bread, but almost certainly not a binding contact with God. In both encounters God wants a binding contract with them. So the Israelites drink and eat, and God obtains their commitment, unwittingly, it seems, to an admixture of miracles and His compendium.

At Shur and at Marah the Israelites learn the essence of God's social structure: "***that you obey God, your Lord, and do what is upright in His eyes, carefully heeding all His commandments, and keeping all His decrees—the compendium of them.*"** *(15:22-26, as above)*

As they soon discover, the compendium is complex indeed, and God's response to tampering with it is almost always swift and painful.

> [13] One morning, still at Sin, they are puzzled by a layer of dew. When it evaporates,[14] there were little grains all over the surface of the desert. [15] The Israelites looked at it, and had no idea what it was. "What is it" they asked one another. Moses said to them, "This is the bread that God is giving you to eat. [16] God's instructions are that each man shall take as much as he needs. There shall be an omer for each person, according to the number of people each man has in his tent." [17] When the Israelites went to do this, some gathered more and some less. [18] But when they measured it with an omer, the one who had taken more did not have any extra, and the one who had taken less did not have too little. They had gathered exactly enough for each one to eat. [19] Moses announced to them, "Let no man leave any over until morning."[20] Some men did not listen to Moses and left a portion over for the morning. It became putrid and maggoty with worms. Moses was angry with [these people]. [21] [The people] gathered it each morning, according to what each person would eat. Then, when the sun became hot, it melted. [22] When Friday came, what they gathered turned out to be a double portion of food, two omers for each person. All the leaders of the community came and reported it to Moses.
> *[6:15-22]*

The worms that turn the bread putrid bespeak God's anger, underscored by that of Moses; anger to be feared—even to be terrified of—and therefore to forestall disobedience most prudently by study of the compendium.

Thus, such study cannot end, in the instance above, with the arrival of the leaders of the community, who have come to learn a few of the laws of the Sabbath. As a practical matter, it can never end, because time is insufficient to fathom it, and because safety depends upon it.

Because the learning curve related to the compendium is remarkably steep; because, as noted, God is adamant about protecting its integrity; and because as it unfolds the Israelites are understandably uncertain of how to placate Him, their fear—even their terror—of the consequence of not placating Him bespeaks, at the least, prudence.

The terror does not appear explicitly until a pivotal moment at Mount Sinai. But it is implicit before that moment occurs. The Israelites do not comment on, but must be deeply shaken by, God's seemingly self-delighted dismemberment of Pharaoh and his cohort, plague by plague, and His annihilation of them at the Red Sea; aware that His power is infinite, whereas their own is by comparison negligible; and that direct interaction with infinite power easily incited to rage should perhaps less often be sought than immersion in His compendium as the measure of obedience. It may, that is to say, seem prudent to suspect that, having witnessed the fatal power unleashed in the plagues, the Israelites do not underestimate the inevitable, unwelcome cost of rousing God's rage.

At the pivotal moment in human history their terror is explicit. When, that is to say, the miracle unfolds upon which, for traditionalist Israelites, history pivots—when God appears on Mount Sinai to irradiate the Israelites with the most precious of His gifts, His compendium—they retreat, terrified, convinced that even overhearing Him intone it would kill them.

Precisely what they overhear is not certain. But their conviction that they will survive only if they overhear as little as possible—preferably nothing—is unshakable.

God's expectation is beyond doubt. He tells Moses, "I will come to you in a thick cloud, so that all the people will hear when I speak to you. They will then believe in you forever" [19:9]. But beyond doubt also, the Israelites desperately prefer silence.

> [15] All the people saw the sounds, the flames, the blast
> of the ram's horn, and the mountain smoking. The peo-
> ple trembled when they saw it, keeping their distance.
> [16] They said to Moses, "You speak to us, and we will
> listen. But let God not speak to us anymore, for we will

die if He does."[17] "Do not be afraid," replied Moses to the people. "God only came to raise you up. His fear will then be on your faces, and you will not sin." [18] The people kept their distance while Moses entered the mist where the Divine was [revealed].
(20:15-18)

That terror does engulf the Israelites at the danger of even overhearing Him is manifest. That their terror deepens as Moses speaks is inaccessible in English translation, but clear in Hebrew, summarized as follows: When the Israelites tell Moses that hearing God will kill them, they back away, each individually (*vah-yam-dew may-ra-chok*). When Moses then assures them that, to the contrary, God intends to protect them against sin, they back away further, as one, as a community completely unified in disbelief (*va-yah-mod may-ra-chok*).

That the pivotal miracle of God's appearance on Mount Sinai will enthrone the compendium as the preferred measure of obedience to Him is foreshadowed by the sudden appearance of a single instance of it, the minutely detailed description of the meal the Israelites must eat on the night they exit Egypt, above; and is established below by the fact that the miracle occurs almost exclusively not to display its stunning self, but to expound the compendium that God will teach to Moses, and that Moses will teach to the Israelites.

Because, as noted above, even the foreshadow of the compendium diminishes narrative, its advent in force from the Revelation at Mount Sinai to the end of the *Five Books* perforce underscores attention to the study of God's Law; taught by God to Moses, beyond doubt enthralled through forty days and nights, and thereafter by Moses to the Israelites, suspicious, at the least, of spiritual elevation.

And that the Israelites suddenly betray study—that God encounters them at the foot of Mount Sinai worshipping a golden calf—that they conclude, on no evidence, that Moses will not be returning—that they disown Moses, God, Mount Sinai, compendium—that they accept Revelation though it may mean death because they are more afraid not to accept it—that to God they prefer an inert idol incapable of interaction with Israelites or with anyone else, a mockery in senseless gold of spiritual aspiration, a lifeless parody they prefer to life, as they always have done—that , as God has known since the beginning of *Genesis,* of a basic, apparently ineradicable defect in them that Moses, who nevertheless loves and protects them, chides them with "From the day you left Egypt until you came here, you have been rebelling against God"[9:8]—that God responds inevitably.

It explodes at once; a cause and effect that, tragically, governs virtually all the remainder of the present study to perforce its end in catastrophe.

Profoundly disgusted by the depravity at the bottom of Mount Sinai, God resolves to destroy the Israelites, and Moses, hardly less infuriated, resolves to punish them without mercy.

Aaron having declared a day of festival,

> [6] getting up early the next morning, [the people] sacrificed burnt offerings and brought peace offerings. The people sat down to eat and drink, and then got up to enjoy themselves. [7] God declared to Moses, "Go down, for the people whom you brought out of Egypt have become corrupt. [8] They have been quick to leave the way I ordered them to follow, and they have made themselves a cast-metal calf. They have bowed down and offered sacrifice to it, exclaiming, "This, Israel, is your god, who brought you out of Egypt." [9] God then said to Moses, "I have observed the people, and they are an unbending group. [10] Now do not try to stop Me when I unleash My wrath against them to destroy them. I will then make you into a great nation."
> *(32:6-10)*

The repudiation of God by the repudiation of His compendium, the essence of His social structure, is total. So the burnt offerings do not honor him. The depravity does not honor Him. The molten calf does not honor Him. The sacrifices do not honor Him. Everything the Israelites say and do disgraces Him, and recalls His regret in *Genesis* soon after He created the world that He resolved to obliterate it, and that He did obliterate it, almost completely.

> [5] God saw that man's wickedness on earth was increasing. Every impulse of his innermost thought was only for evil, all day long. [6] God regretted that He had made man on earth, and He was pained to His very core. [7] God said, "I will obliterate humanity that I have created from the face of the earth—man, livestock, land animals, and birds in the sky. I regret that I created them."
> **(Genesis, 6:5-7)**

Similarly disgusted by the degenerate mob at Mount Sinai, He decides to annihilate it and to replace it with progeny of Moses.

> [7] God declared to Moses, "Go down, for the people whom you brought out of Egypt have become corrupt. [8] They have been quick to leave the way that I ordered them to follow, and they have made themselves a cast-metal calf. They have bowed down and offered to it, exclaiming, "This, Israel, is your god, who brought you out of Egypt." [9] God then said to Moses, "I have observed the people, and they are an unbending group. [10] Now do not try to stop Me when I unleash My wrath against them to destroy them. I will then make you into a great nation."
> **(32:7-10)**

The indictment unimpeachable, the rage begins at once. The Israelites abandon Him on no evidence that Moses abandoned them. Nowhere had they been told that Moses would return after forty days and nights; nor had Moses been told. "They have been quick to leave the way I ordered them to follow"—they abandon as quickly as they can God's compendium—because from their first encounter with it, at Mount Sinai, spiritual elevation has terrified them, because it necessitates the unremitting study of God, essentially the study of how to love, and be loved by, God, whereas death necessitates nothing but supine existence and the degeneracy that once attended all of Noah's generation but, for a time, himself, and that at once attends the Israelites who abandon God at Mount Sinai.

Enraged by the abandonment in general, and by the degeneracy in particular, God appears to respond as He has done to all disobedience thus far: He crushes it. Though Moses pleads successfully against annihilation, His love of Abraham, Isaac and Jacob, God decrees a slaughter, His facilitators the Levites:

> [26] Moses stood up at the camp's entrance and announced, "Whoever is for God, join Me!" All the Levites gathered around him. [27] He said to them, "This is what God, Lord of Israel, says: Let each man put on his sword, and go from one gate to the other in the camp. Let each one kill [all of those involved in the idolatry], even his own brother, close friend, or relative." [28] The Levites did as Moses had ordered, and approximately 3000 people were killed that day.
> *(32:26-28)*

And to complement the three thousand, God dispatches almost at once a plague of unnumbered deaths [32:35].

But then the almost unimaginable abatement in God occurs: almost in mid-tirade, He responds to reason in Moses:

> [9] God then said to Moses, "I have observed the people, and they are an unbending group. [10]. Now do not try to stop Me when I unleash my wrath against them to destroy them. I will then make you into a great nation."
> *(32:9-10)*

The response of Moses is two-fold: that destroying the Israelites will tarnish His reputation for power among the Egyptians, and that dishonor His promise to the Israelites as a nation:

> [11] Moses began to plead before God his Lord. He said, "O God, why unleash Your wrath against Your people, whom You brought out of Egypt with great power and a show of force? [12] Why should Egypt be able to say that You took them out with evil intentions, to kill them in the hill country, And wipe them out from the face of the earth. Withdraw Your display of anger, and refrain

from doing evil to your people. [13] Remember your servants, Abraham, Isaac and Jacob. You swore to them by Your very essence, and declared that you would make descendants as numerous as the stars of the sky, giving their descendants the land, so that they would be able to occupy forever. [14] God refrained from doing the evil that He planned for His people.
(32:11-14)

That Moses' response is impeccable both in substance and in form establishes that he is thinking clearly. And that God cordons His rage establishes that, during an unprecedented interaction, He subordinates emotion to reason, and therefore refrains from inflicting evil upon the Israelites.

The same subordination is evident when God assures them that they will reach the land He has chosen for them; but has decided that to protect against a resurgence of His rage, their journey to it will be led, not by Him, but by an angel.

[1] God declared to Moses, "You and the people you took out of Egypt will have to leave this place and go to the land regarding which I swore to Abraham, Isaac and Jacob that I would give it to their descendants. [2] I will send an angel ahead of you, and drive out the Canaanites, Amorites, Hittites, Perizites, Hivites and Yebustes. [3] [You will thus go to a land flowing with milk and honey. However, I will not go with you, since you are an unbending people, and I may destroy you along the way." [4] When they heard this bad news, the people began to mourn. They stopped wearing jewelry. [5] God told Moses to say to the Israelites, "You are an unbending people, In just one second I can go among you and utterly destroy you. Now take off your jewelry. And I will know what to do with you."
(33:1-5)

He will not destroy them; absent further profound dereliction, their nadir apparently forgiven, He will lead them home; disburdened Himself of some measure of rage.

Tragically, that is not what happens. To the contrary; *in **Le-viticus***, the first of three remaining sections of the ***Five Books***, the first of three profoundly destructive explosions suddenly occurs: an attempt to create an interval, perhaps even a community, rooted in productivity and benevolence is stillborn by a sudden outburst of rage in God; In ***Numbers,*** the second of the three such sections, a sudden plague of cowardice explodes in almost all of the Israelites, undermining the Exodus ***per se***; and in ***Deuteronomy***, the third of such sections, almost all of the Israelites abandon God's compendium, in a catastrophic outburst thereby abandoning each his essence, his nation, his God; in retaliation for which action, God almost resolves to abandon the Israelites.

For the section of ***Leviticus*** of interest to the present study to prosper—indeed, to approach religious ecstasy—three conditions must exist: a *Tabernacle* must be almost ready to function; virtually nothing must be required of the Israelites; and God must act throughout in a fashion foreign to Him in *Genesis* and in *Exodus*. The first and second conditions are met completely. So also is the third; except, tragically, suddenly enraged, God smothers surpassing delight in hideous terror.

Because the wonderment of the *Tabernacle* is in its exactitude, and it hides no dangers, the sample of it below is sufficient comment:

> [1] Make the tabernacle out of ten large tapestries consisting of twined linen, and blue-sky, dark red, and crimson [wool], with a pattern of cherubs woven into them. [2] Each cherub shall be 28 cubits long and 4 cubits wide, with each tapestry the same size. [3] The [first] five tapestries shall be sewn together. [4] Make loops of blue-sky wool at the end of the innermost tapestry of the first group. Do the same on the edge of the innermost tapestry of the second group [5] Place 50 loops on the one tapestry, and 50 on the edge of the tapestry of the second group. [The two sets of loops shall be made so that] the loops are exactly opposite one another. [6] Make 50 golden fasteners. The two [groups of] tapestries will then be able to be joined together, so the tabernacle will be

one piece. [7] Make sheets of goat's wool to serve as a tent over the tabernacle. There shall be 11 such sheets, [8] and each sheet shall be 30 cubits long, and 4 cubits wide. All 11 sheets must be the same size.
(***Exodus, 26:1-8***)

The wonderment of God, that turns out to hide fatal dangers, is that at His first appearance He is astoundingly approachable, and apparently intent on enhancing the lives of the Israelites, as His opening address shows:

[1] God called to Moses, speaking to him from the Communion Tent. He said, [2] "Speak to the Israelites, and tell them the following: When one of you brings a mammal as an offering to God, the sacrifice must be taken from the cattle, sheep or goats. [3] If the sacrifice is a burnt offering taken from the cattle, it must be an unblemished male. One must bring it of his own free will to the entrance of the Communion Tent, before God. [4] He shall press his hands on the head of the burnt offering, and it shall then be accepted as an atonement for him. [5] He shall slaughter a young bull before God. Aaron's sons, the priests, shall then bring forth the blood, dashing it on all sides of the altar that is in front of the Communion Tent entrance.[6] He shall skin the burnt offering and cut it into pieces. [7] Aaron's sons shall place fire on the altar, and arrange wood on the fire. [8] Aaron's sons shall then arrange the cut pieces, the head, and the fatty intestinal membrane that is on the altar fire.]9] The inner organs and legs, however, must [first] be scrubbed with water. The priest shall thus burn the entire [animal] on the altar as a completely burnt fire offering to God, an appeasing fragrance."
(***1:1-9***)

Though—a rare event in *Genesis* and *Exodus*—the suppliant in the statement above admits, and presumably regrets, that he has sinned, God does not order him to do or to say anything not prompted by his own will. He need not offer a sacrifice. If he does choose to offer one (in which animals are sacrificed), God, acting through His ordained priests, arranges it, without reprimand, in the *Tabernacle* in a manner that cleanses the suppliant, who, except for slaughtering an animal, typically does none of the work involved. In cognate situations, though sacrifices must be brought, and specific details may vary, the same template is commonly used.

In all relevant situations, the comfort and dignity of the suppliant are respected. No one orders him to do anything. He does almost no work. And his sin is voided.

Because the sacrifices discussed require that the *Tabernacle* be completely functioning, when it is almost prepared for consecration God commands that the anointed priests, Aaron and his four sons:

> [33] "Do not leave the entrance of the Communion Tent for seven days, until your period of inauguration is complete. [34] God has commanded that whatever was done on this day must be done [all seven days] to atone for you. [35] Remain at the Communion Tent's entrance day and night for seven days. You will thus keep God's charge, and not die, since this is what God has commanded." [36] Aaron and his sons did all these things, just as God had commanded through Moses.
> *(8:33-36)*

The priests' reward, and that of all of the Israelites, for the priests' scrupulous obedience to the commandment above, is astounding: a number of sacrifices offered on the eighth day during which God promises, He "will reveal Himself to you" [9:4], and "God's glory will be revealed to you" [9:6]—a transcendental promise that He keeps:

> [23] Moses and Aaron went into the Communion Tent, and when they came out they blessed the people. God's glory was then revealed to all the people. [24] Fire came forth from before God and consumed the burnt offering and the choice parts on the altar. When the people saw this, they raised their voices in praise, and threw themselves on their faces.
> *(10:23-24)*

Because until the day under discussion, the first in which the *Tabernacle* would function completely, rituals requiring it were discussed, but not performed. Therefore the day under discussion attracted the entire nation as to a holiday. Tragically, however, without warning, the ecstasy of thousands who had done nothing wrong was shattered, a profoundly impressive family was ravaged, the aspiration for benevolent and productive co-existence between the Israelites and God disintegrated, and the dreary relation between them of disobedience and punitive rage that had governed them from Eden to the opening of *Leviticus* was restored, to govern the rest of the *Five Books* as, the aspirational moment having came to nothing, it has always governed—because of God's response to a mistake made by two of Aaron' sons:

> [1] Aaron's sons Nadav and Avihu each took his fire pan, placed fire on it, and then incense on it. They offered it before God, [but it was] unauthorized fire, which [God] had not instructed them [to offer]. [2] Fire came forth from before God, and it consumed them, so that they died before God. [3] Moses said to Aaron, "This is exactly what God meant when He said, 'I will be sanctified by those close to Me, and I will thus be glorified.' Aaron remained silent. [4] Moses summoned Mishael and Eltzafan, the sons of Aaron's uncle Uziel, and he said to them, "Bring forth your close relatives and carried from inside the sanctuary. [Bring them] outside the camp. [5] They came forth and carried [Nadav and Avihu] outside the camp, in their tunics, as Moshe had said. [6] Moshe said to Aaron and his sons, "Do not go without a haircut, and do not tear your vestments; otherwise you will die, bringing divine wrath upon the entire community. As far as your brothers are concerned, let the entire family mourn for the ones whom God burned. [7] Do not leave the entrance of the Communion Tent lest you die, because God's anointing oil is still upon you. "They did as Moshe had said.
>
> *(10:1-7)*

The sudden grief of the thousands for the loss of the ecstasy is manifest. That Nadav and Avihu are impressive is affirmed in various contexts. When Moses begins his ascent of Mount Sinai, he is accompanied, in Exodus 24:9-11, only by Aaron, his sons Nadav and Avihu, and seventy of Israel's elders, and only they see a vision of the God of Israel that not even Aaron's other two sons, Ithamar and Eleazer, are privileged to experience. Together with their father and their brothers, Nadav and Avihu are elevated above all other Israelites, including Moses, to the priesthood, which is reserved, in Exodus 28:1-29:37, 40:14, in perpetuity for them and their descendants alone. They are not implicated in their father's appeasement, in Exodus 32:-25, that occasions the sin of the Golden Calf. They participate in the retribution God exacts in 32:26-29, for that sin. And in Exodus 29:1-46, in an elaborate ceremony that unfolds over seven days, together with their father and their brothers, they are consecrated.

Aaron's preeminence is underscored by his centrality as High Priest at the consecration of the *Tabernacle*. His pride as the father of the only four others priests cannot be difficult to imagine; that he expected catastrophe, that prudence would argue silence when it struck, that burial rites for his sons would be restricted, that his two remaining sons might not survive the day no doubt was impossible to imagine until they materialized.

And far worse, the Israelites are terrified, one moment in spiritual elevation with God, the next, God ranting at disobedience, and warning that other brothers might yet die—in effect proclaiming that the interval—to say nothing of a community, of benevolence, having barely begun—has suddenly disappeared; as it turns out, never to reappear in the *Five Books*.

The hideous unfolding of the day of Consecration complete, the interest in sacrifice of *Leviticus* recedes abruptly because, though it is referenced often enough to be kept in mind, it contends for attention with a formidable list of matters completely or predominantly related to the compendium.

The relevant list includes dietary laws, sexual laws, laws about leprosy, laws about female discharges, male discharges, menstruation, holiness, forbidden practices, priestly laws, laws about the High Priest, blemished priests, priestly purity, about Sabbath, about the sabbatical year, the jubilee year, blasphemy, redemption of land in walled cities, houses in walled cities, helping others, Israelite slaves, gentile slaves—a torrent of additions to God's compendium, in no discernable order, all engrossing—if not in intent, certainly in effect distracts, in some measure at least some attention from sacrifice.

The first ten concerns in **Numbers** provide no hint of the cataclysm that has begun to shatter the *Five Books*. A consensus of the Israelites is taken. Each tribe is assigned its place in the total community, when stationary and when moving, laws are added to the compendium that govern a woman accused by her husband of adultery, a Nazir, the sacrifices offered in the *Tabernacle* on specific days, and so on. And most of the turmoil that follows those concerns—the familiar whining of the Israelites, the sudden revolt of Moses' sister, Miriam—seems manageable. But the ten hither-to illustrious Israelites debased, as spies, into dangerously infectious cowards imperiling God's intention must be punished sternly, and at once.

And they are. When they finish their report on the homeland God has chosen for the Israelites, the depth of their perfidy—and its poisonous spread *en masse*—their demand that the choice be obviated, because, they have concluded, it is beyond their strength—beyond God's strength—that, in short, the Exodus be abandoned, utterly and at once—is inescapable; as is His rage, followed swiftly by punishment fierce almost beyond imagining:

> [27] They gave the following report: "We came to the land where you sent us, and it is indeed flowing with milk and honey, as you can see from its fruit.[28] However, the people the people living in the land are aggressive, and the cities are large and well fortified. We also saw the giants' descendants there. [29] Amalek lives in the Negev lives in the Negev area, the Hittites, Yebusites and Amorites live in the hills, and the Canaanites near the sea and on the banks of the Jordan." [30] Caleb tried to quiet the people for Moses. "We must go forth and occupy the land," he said. "We can do it!" [31] "We cannot go forward against those people." [32] They began to

speak badly about the land that they had explored. They told the Israelites, "The land that we crossed to explore is a land that consumes its inhabitants. All the men we saw were huge. [33] While we were there, we saw the titans. They were sons of the giant, who descended from the [original] titans. We were like tiny grasshoppers! That's all that we were in their eyes." [1] The entire community raised a hubhub and began to shout. That night, the people wept. [2] All the Israelites complained to Moses and Aaron. The entire community was saying, "We wish we had died in Egypt! We should have died in this desert! [3] Why is God bringing us to this land to die by the sword? Our wives and children will be captives! It would be best to go back to Egypt!"[4] The people started saying to one another, "Let's appoint a [new] leader and go back to Egypt." [5] Moses and Aaron fell on their faces before the whole assembled Israelite community. [6] Among the men who had explored the land, Joshua son of Nun and Caleb son of Yefuneh tore their clothes in grief. [7] They said to the whole Israelite community, "The land through we passed in our explorations is a very, very good land! [8] If God is satisfied with us and brings us to this land, He can give it to us—a land flowing with milk and honey. [9] But don't rebel against God! Don't be afraid of the people in the land! They have lost their protection and shall be our prey! God is with us, so don't be afraid!" [10] The whole community was threatening to stone them to death when God's glory suddenly appeared at the Communion Tent before all the Israelites.
(*13:27-14:10*)

In response to a plea from Moses, God consents not to annihilate the Israelites. Because, however, He is not this time to be placated, He decrees the following hideous punishment:

[28] Tell them as follows: "As I am Life, it is God's solemn declamation that I will make your accusations against Me come true. [29] Because you have complained about Me, you corpses will fall in this desert. [This will happen to] your complete tally, everyone over twenty years old who was counted. [30] [My oath is that] you will not come

into the land regarding which I swore with a raised hand that I would let you live in undisturbed. The only exceptions will be Caleb [son of Yefuneh]and Joshua [son of Nun). [31] You said that your children will be taken captive, but they will be the ones I will bring [there], so that they will know the land that you rejected. [32] You, however, will fall as copses in the desert . [33] Your children will be herded [from place to place] in the desert for forty years, paying for your indiscretion until the last of your corpses lie here in the desert. [34] [The punishment] shall parallel the number of days that you spent exploring the land. There were forty days, and there shall be one year for each day, a total of forty years until your sin is forgiven. You will then know how I act. [35] I, God, have spoken, and [there is no way] I will not do this to the entire evil community that has banded against me. They will end their lives in this desert, and here is where they will die." [36] The men whom Moses sent to explore the land, and who returned and complained about it to the entire community, slandering the land, [were punished immediately]. [37] The men who had given a bad report about the land thus died before God in the plague. [38] Among the men who went to explore the land, only Joshua (son of Nun) and Caleb (son of Yefuneh) remained alive.
(14:28-38)

Almost all of **Deuteronomy** (including a prologue not included in the present study) is narrated by Moses, on the appropriate relation between God and the Israelites. But almost immediately after that narration ends in a soothing, humane discourse, culled from the narrative, it is overwhelmed by an outburst by God on the anathema of virtually all Israelites abandoning His compendium and therefore, in effect, Himself; an outburst so sudden, so astounding, so destructive, it is almost too odious to hear or even to read.

The narrative begins by underscoring the indispensability of God's compendium, then establishes by presenting excerpts from it (chosen at random) how God requires Israelites to live, and the fitness of Moses to teach it to them.

> [1] "Now, Israel, listen to the rules and laws that I am teaching you to do, so that you will remain and come to occupy the land that God, Lord of your fathers, is giving you. [2] Do not add to the word that I am commanding you, and do not subtract from it. You must keep all the commandments of God your Lord, which I am instructing you. [3] You have seen with your own eyes what God did at Baal Peor. God your Lord annihilated every person among you who followed Baal Peor. [4] Only you, the ones who remained attached to God your Lord are alive today. [5] See! I have taught you ruses as God my Lord has commanded me, [that you] will be able to keep them in the land to which you are coming and which you will be occupying.
>
> [6] Safeguard and keep [these rules], since this is your wisdom and understanding in the eyes of the nations. They will hear all these rules and say, "This great nation is certainly a wise and understanding people."[7] What nation is so great that they have God close to it, as God our Lord is, whenever we call Him? [8] What nation is so great that they have such righteous rules and laws like this entire Torah that I am presenting before you today? [9] Only take heed and watch yourselves very carefully, so that you do not forget the things your eyes saw. Do not let [this memory] leave your hearts, all the days of your lives."
>
> *(4:1-9)*

> [29] "Be careful to do what God your Lord has commanded you, not turning to the right or left. [30] Follow the entire way that God your has commanded you, so that you may live and do well, enduring for a long time on the land that you are going to occupy."
>
> *(5:29-30)*

> "You must safeguard and keep the entire mandate I am prescribing to you today. You will then survive, flourish,

and come to occupy the land that God swore to your
fathers."
(8:1)

"Keep God's commandments and decrees that I am pre-
scribing for you today, so that good will be yours.[14]
The heaven, the heaven of heaven, the earth and everything in it, all belong to God![15] Still, it was only to your
ancestors that God developed a closeness. He loved them
and therefore chose you, their descendants, from among
all nations, just as the situation is today.
[16] Remove the barriers from your heart and do not
remain so stubborn any more!"
(10:12-16)

"Love God your Lord, and safeguard His trust, His decrees, laws and commandments, for all time."
(11:1)

"I call heaven and earth as witnesses for you today that
you will then quickly perish from the land that you are
crossing the Jordan to occupy. You will not remain there
very long, for you will be utterly destroyed."
(4:26).

[30] "When you are in distress and all these things have
happened to you, you will finally return to [31] God
your Lord and obey Him. God your Lord is a merciful
Power, and He will not abandon you or destroy you; He
will not forget the oath He made upholding your fathers'
covenant."
(4:30-31)

The total statement by Moses summarized above reflects
accurately his humane nature, and apparently his ideal fitness to
lead his fellow Israelites. He loves them unshakably. He knows,
and underscores to them, that they can survive only by clinging to
God and to His compendium, the essence of His social structure.
He believes unshakably that God wants them to do so, will help
them to do so, and will deal mercifully when they struggle or fail to
do so, because they are rebellious, wicked, sinful, and worries that
they may chose death, not life. He underscores that they are free

not to do so; that life is neither a far-distant nor a difficult choice; that God has chosen only them as His special nation; that because He revers their obedient lineage He will never abandon or destroy them. And he is measured, reassuring, and reasonable throughout.

The outburst by God, occasioned by His rage at the gradual abandonment of compendium discussed in detail above, is neither reassuring nor measured, God and Moses being as different in presentation as in character. God's interest in communicants less obedient than Abraham is nil. His assertiveness is as salient as is the humility of Moses. From first appearance to last He demands obedience, and is typically furious—and prone to imposing irreversible punishments—even death—to even the most loyal of His servants; as is demonstrated below when He decrees that Moses will die while his fellow Israelites cross the Jordan River; his punishment for an apparently immaterial blunder that offends Him; the only such blunder that mars forty years of otherwise flawless service with the vengeance-suffused remainder of the book:

> [7] God spoke to Moses, saying, [8] "Take the staff, and you and Aaron assemble the community Speak to the cliff in their presence, and it will give forth its water. You will thus bring forth water from the cliff, and allow the community and their livestock to drink." [9] Moses took the staff from before God as he had been instructed
> [10] Moses and Aaron then assembled the congregation before the cliff. "Listen now, you rebels!" shouted Moses. "Shall we produce water for you from this cliff?" [11] With that, Moses raised his hand, and struck the cliff twice with his staff. A huge amount of water gushed out, and the community and their animals were able to drink.
> [12] God said to Moses and Aaron, "You did not have enough faith in Me to sanctify Me in the presence of the Israelites! Therefore, you shall not bring this assembly to the land that I have given you."
> *(Numbers 20:7-12*

And when the day for the journey to the land arrives, (the day Moses dies) God keeps His word:

[16] God said to Moses, "When you go and lie with your ancestors, this nation will rise up and stray after the alien gods of the land into which they are coming. They will thus abandon Me and violate the covenant that I have made with them. [17] I will then display anger against them and abandon them. I will hide My face from them and they will be [their enemies'] prey. Beset by many evils and troubles, they will say, 'It is because my God is no longer with me that these evils have befallen us.' [18] On that day I will utterly hide My face because of all the evil that they have done in turning to alien gods. [19] Now write for yourselves this song and teach it to the Israelites. Make them memorize it, so that this song will be a witness for the Israelites. [20] When I bring them to the land flowing with milk and honey that I promised their ancestors, they will eat, be satisfied, and live in luxury. They will then turn to foreign gods and worship them, despising Me and violating My covenant. [21] When they are beset by many evils and troubles, this song shall testify like a witness, since it will not be forgotten by their descendants. I know their inclinations by what they are doing right now, even before I have brought them to the promised land." [22] On that day, Moses wrote down this song, and taught it to the Israelites. [23] God also gave Joshua orders, saying, "Be strong and brave, since you will bring the Israelites to the land I promised them, and I will be with you." [24] Moses finished writing the words of this Torah to the very end. [25] Moses then gave orders to the Levites who carried the Ark of God's covenant, saying [26]" Take this Torah scroll see and place it to the side of the ark [27] I am aware of your rebellious spirit [27] I am aware of your rebellious spirit and your stubbornness. Even while I am here alive with you, you are rebelling against God. What will you do when I am dead? [28] Gather to me all the elders of your tribes and your law enforcers and I will proclaim these words to them. I will bring heaven and earth as witnesses to them [29] I know that after I die, you will become corrupt and turn away from the path that I have prescribed for you. You will eventually be beset with evil, since you will have done evil in God's eyes, angering Him with the work

of your hands. [30] Moses then proclaimed the words of this song to the entire assembly of Israel until it was completed.
(31:16-30)

Because the Israelites have abandoned Him when they wish to repent, He will hide His face utterly from them. And the mode of His vengeance is fixed: He will dictate to Moses, and every Israelite must memorize, the song that will not only debase them for deficiencies narrated above in *Leviticus* and *Numbers,* but exonerate Himself of all fault in all inexorable, evil imminent.

That on the day of his death, with almost his last words, after forty years of service to God never before or after paralleled or imagined, Moses is commanded to enunciate before his nation a failure he incorrectly imagines his own, and that is certain to torture him, perhaps defies understanding. And that the members of the nation excoriated by the song—as dreadful a song as ever rendered—will be battered by it into repentance is a distant hope, not an expectation.

The prelude to it is God's repetition four times in quick succession that the song is His witness against the Israelites: "This song will be a witness for [against] the Israelites." [31:19] It will testify for [against] them "like a witness" [31:21], a scroll of the Torah will be left "as a witness." (31:26) I will bring heaven and earth as witnesses for [against] them" [31:28].

And the song is venomous: utterly devoid of consolation for the Israelites, consumed in fury, excoriation, disgust, the words uttered above and below a hideous threat fulfilled; to all appearances, His Chosen Nation abandoned by their God.
[each statement below summarizes some past of the song]

"I am perfect—the generation is destructive, warped, twisted ungrateful, unwise—unfair to Me

[4] The deeds of the Mighty One are perfect, for all His ways are just. He is a faithful God, never unfair; righteous and moral is He. [5] Destruction is His children's not His own, you warped and twisted generation.[6] Is this the way you repay God, you ungrateful, unwise

nation? Is He not your father, your Master the One made and established you?"
(32: 4-6)

"You have abandoned, ignored, offended me
I am angry, jealous

[15] Jeshurun thus became fat, and rebelled. You grew fat, thick and gross. [The nation] abandoned the God who made it, and spurned the Mighty One who was its support. [16] They provoked His jealousy with alien practices; made Him angry with vile deeds. [17] They sacrificed to demons who were non- gods, deities they never knew. These were new things, recently arrived, which their fathers would never consider. [18] You thus ignored the" Mighty One who bore you; forgot the Power who delivered you. [19] When God saw this, He was offended, provoked by His sons and daughters. [20] He said: I will hide My face from them, and see what will be their end. They are a generation which reverses itself, and cannot be trusted. They have been faithless to me with a non-God, angering Me with their meaningless acts. Now I will be unfaithful to them with a non-nation, provoking them with a nation devoid of gratitude."
(32:15-20)

"I am so angry I would have exterminated them, if I
had been able take credit as God for having done so—or
consumed them by famine, by fever, by plague."

[22] "My anger has kindled a fire, burning to the lowest depths. Consume the land and its crops, setting fire to the foundations of mountains. [23] I will heap evil upon them, striking them with my arrows.[24] [They will be] bloated with famine, consumed by fever, cut down by bitter plague. I will send against them fanged beasts, with venomous creatures who crawl in the dust. [25] Outside, the sword will butcher boys, girls, infants, white-headed elders, while inside, there shall be terror. [26] I was prepared to exterminate them, make their memory vanish from among mankind. [27] I was concerned that their enemies would be provoked, and their attackers

alienated, so they would say, "Our superior power and not God was what caused all this."
(*32:22-27*)

"None of them will escape My retribution

[31] Their powers are not like our Mighty One, although our enemies sit in judgment. [32] But their vine is from the vine of Sodom and the shoot of Gomorrah. Their grapes are poison grapes; their grape cluster is bitterness to them. [33] Their vine is serpents' vine, like the poison of the dreadful cobra. [34] But it is concealed with Me for the future, sealed up in My treasury [35] I have vengeance and retribution, waiting for their foot to slip. Their day of disaster is near, and their time is about to come. God will then take up the cause of His people, and comfort His servants. He will have seen that their power is gone, with nothing left to keep or abandon. [37] [God] will then say: Where is their God, the power in which they trusted?
[38] [Where are the gods] who ate the fat of their sacrifices and drank the wine of their libations? Let them now help you! Let them be your protector! [39] But now see! It is I! I am the [only] One! There are no [other] gods with Me! I kill and give life! If I crushed, I will heal! But there is no protection from My power! [40] I lift My hand to heaven and say: I am life forever."
(*32:31-40*)

I will rescue the deserving of My Nation

[41] I will whet My lightning sword and grasp judgment in My hand. I will bring vengeance against *My* foes, and repay those who hated Me. [42] I will make My arrows drunk with blood, my s(word consuming flesh. The enemy's first punishment will be the blood of the slain and wounded. [43] Let the tribes of His nation sing praise, for He will avenge His servants' blood. He will bring vengeance upon His foes, and reconcile people [to] His land.
(*32:41-43*)

At virtually the end of the *Five Books*, a short statement of closure appears, technically a *sedra, in Hebrew, one of the units into which the Book is often divided,* that rouses reasonable speculation about why *God's excoriation of the Israelites, above, and a blessing bestowed by Moses, below, are juxtaposed.* The speculation posits that the excoriation is so terrifying, it requires a palliative; that, though dying, Moses provides, by teaching the Israelites, first individually, then as a nation, not to fear and shun the compendium as a path to catastrophe, but to embrace it as a path unto God. For example:

To Levi, he said: Your Urim and Thumim belong to Your pious one. You tested him at Massah, and contended with him at the Waters of Dispute.
(33:8)

To Benjamin he said: God's beloved one shall dwell securely beside Him. [God] protects him all day long and dwells among his slopes.
(33:12)

To Joseph he said: His land is a blessing of God, with the sweetness of the heaven's dew, and the waters that lie below, the sweetness of the sun's yield, the sweetness of moon's crop, the best of the ancient mountains, the sweetness of the eternal hills, the sweetness of the land and its fullness, and the favor of the One who dwells in the thorn-bush.
(33:13-16)

And to the Israelites as a nation he said:
Happy are you Israel! Who is like you? [You are] a nation delivered by God, the shield that helps you, and your triumphant sword.]
(33:29)

www.ingramcontent.com/pod-product-compliance
Lightning Source LLC
Chambersburg PA
CBHW070737030726
47601CB00001B/43